Manifest a Better Life with God

Use Your Inherent God Nature, which Includes Law of Attraction

Michael LeBlanc, MSW, LCSW

ISBN-13: 978-0692845127

ISBN-10: 0692845127

1

TABLE OF CONTENTS

Acknowledgements

Over the years, various spiritual teachings have resonated with me while others have not. I have come to trust these feelings and encourage others to do the same. This way, you are guided from within. The following are some spiritual teachings that resonate with me: Earnest Holmes (*The Science of Mind* and other writings), *A Course in Miracles* and study group, Jack Boland lectures, *The Teachings of Abraham* and workshop (Jerry and Ester Hicks), *The I AM Discourses* by Godfré Ray King, various Psalms and other passages from the Bible, writings by Neville Goddard, Native American teachings and workshops, writings on energy work, such as *Hands of Light* by Barbara Brennan and Reiki workshops, writings by Wayne Dyer, Ken Wilber, Caroline Myss (books and workshop), Shakti Gawain (books and workshop), David R. Hawkins, Neil Douglas-Klotz (*The Hidden Gospel*), Joe Dispenza, Joe Vitali (*Zero Limits*), Ho'oponopono workshop, Father Thomas Keating (teachings on Centering Prayer and silent retreats), and many more.

I genuinely wish to thank each one of these spiritual teachers for the part they've played in my spiritual journey. Thanks also to Tim and Barbara Cook with

Church of Conscious Harmony and the tremendous role you've played in my relationship with God.

Many close friends and family over the years also have been part of my journey, and my husband Mark Wright and I thank and send constant love and blessings to each of them always.

Thanks to a special group of friends that help with editing my initial versions of the book (Dana, Dona, Louise, Mark, Monique, Tamara and Wayne).

Thanks to Joe Vitale's Authorship Program and my writing coach, Adam Mortimer with Achieve Today, Tonya Simpson, my editor, and Alan Clements, for his artwork and cover design.

And thanks, God, for giving us yourself, for this mysterious thing we call life, and for teaching me how to play with you and participate in life in a meaningful way.

Introduction

You and I are an expression of God and God consciousness in a very literal sense; therefore, we have what I call an inherent God nature. God consciousness, our inherent God nature, the vibrational nature of consciousness, physical life (including you and me), our emotions, law of attraction, manifesting a better life, are all intertwined and related. All of it can be applied and used to manifest better conditions in your life.

Many times in my life, the various spiritual teachings I have studied and practiced over the past 30 years (as mentioned in the acknowledgments) worked and I have manifested and allowed better conditions in my life, and others times they didn't seem to work. So I figured that if I have issues manifesting better conditions in my life I should go to the expert, God.

This book is literally a personal *conversation with God* about how to manifest better conditions in our lives and figure out why prayers, visualizations, affirmations and other methods don't *seem* to work at times and what to do about it.

I know there are folks who struggle with God and feel separate and unworthy. I've been one of these folks, and I wrote Part 1 of this book, "Your Inherent God Nature," as a way to help end this struggle. It is also about our relationship with God, our inherent God nature, the vibrational nature of God consciousness and the role our emotions play in helping us know how aligned or misaligned we are with our inherent God nature. These aspects relate to manifesting better conditions in our lives.

I wrote Part 2 of this book, "Create and Manifest with God," to provide tips and nuances on how to deliberately use our inherent God nature (which includes law of attraction) to manifest better conditions in our lives. Part 2 also explores three specific reasons why manifesting might not be working out for you and what to do about it. I attempted to write only Part 2, but Part 1 kept wanting "in," and you really can't do Part 2 without Part 1, so I wrote both.

Although I have been studying and practicing various spiritual teachings for 30 years, I guess you could call me a self-taught student of spirituality. I was raised Catholic, but God really wasn't meaningful to me in any particular way until the 1980s, when I was in my early 20s.

In my 20s I thought perhaps I might become a priest, and I spent time with different Catholic orders exploring my options. I ended up not becoming a priest, and went into the field of social work instead.

Even though I chose not to be a priest, God and spirituality have always remained significant, constant and a genuine passion of mine. God and I began as two separate beings, God "up there" and me. Then God became a God "within" instead of "up there" but still remained separate and, to some degree, still a concept and not real. Funny how you can believe in God but at the same time not really realize that God is real. This was one of my many talents. As God and I continued, God within me became "real" and not just a concept, and God became God consciousness, all consciousness, instead of a "being."

I've come to experience God and understand that I am, we are, all physical conditions are, an expression of God consciousness. And we can and are welcome to participate with God and use our inherent God nature and God consciousness to manifest a better life for ourselves. Let this book be one of your guides on how to *know* God more and to manifest a better life. If you want to learn more about me and how to manifest a better life using your inherent God nature, go to my website, CreateWithConsciousness.com.

A small prayer before you begin and join me in my conversation with God:

"God, ignite these words with well-being, relief and peace for any who struggle with you and doubt whether you love them. Let all who read this know that your love for us is immense and always. There truly is nothing we can do or have ever done that alters that. And let all the nuances we share within these pages truly uplift and help others manifest better conditions in their lives." Amen.

Chapter One

God, Why Isn't It Working?

"God, what the heck? I pray and practice Centering Prayer. I visualize, I study spiritual teachings, I meditate, I understand law of attraction, I journal, I go on silent retreats, I do energy work. I've tried breath work and sweat lodges. I attend lectures and workshops with spiritual teachers, you name it, but sometimes these seem to work and other times nothing, nada, no change, even years later!!" This is me whining to God when certain conditions do not manifest; when certain prayers are not answered...like helping me fix issues with money and debt. Things improve. They don't. They improve. They don't.

Welcome to my prayer time with God. I am sitting comfortably in a chair in my home office. It is early morning and still dark outside, quiet and still. The sound of a prayer bowl ringing is fading into the background as I enter into prayer with God. If you saw me right now I'd look pretty peaceful, but inwardly I'm not feeling peaceful, and God and I are about to have a chat. Again. I do not find that prayer and peacefulness always go hand in hand, but I always find that I leave a bit better off than when I start.

I realize that these days a lot of folks call God Source, Universe, and many, many different names, but calling God "God" still works for me.

So I ask God, "Okay, so how do you do it? How do you manifest conditions and consistently get the results you want?" I figure if I have questions about my car, I go to the best mechanic I can find; I ask an expert. If I have questions about manifesting better conditions in my life and praying effectively, I ask the source that creates universes; I ask the expert, God.

Silence for a moment, and then I hear God say the following:

- "Everything exists in God consciousness. Everything is God consciousness. I create in, with, and through this consciousness.
- I create by knowing, not by hoping, believing, pleading, begging, bargaining, or worrying.
- I am allness, whole and complete.
- I do not manifest or create life from a place of lack or need.
- I manifest and create all life from a place of wholeness and completeness.
- This means that I manifest life—physical conditions—for joy of life, for love of life, for pleasure of life and actually for the sheer fun of life, the fun of creating and for the sheer appreciation of the thing itself. This includes

the manifestation of each and every one of you."

God continues, "When you attempt to manifest better conditions in your life through prayer or visualizing, you will be more effective if you

- "Remember that you are dealing with consciousness and not with conditions.
- Start from an inner place of knowing that what you desire or pray for is done. This means pray and visualize from a place of wholeness and completeness, not from a place of need and lack.
- Because you are dealing with consciousness, the inner places of wholeness/completeness and need/lack are vibrationally different and will emotionally feel different to you. This impacts and influences the power of your prayer and visualizations."

God can read the look on my face and knows that I have tons of questions about each one of these ideas and that I want to have a better understanding of it all. "We will spend more time going over this," He says to me.

"But God, when I pray or visualize to manifest a better condition it is usually because I lack something or need something, like money, for example."

"I understand that physically it appears to you that you lack something, but vibrationally and spiritually in nonphysical consciousness you do not truly lack anything. You have only manifested the condition of lack. But within your inherent God nature there is no such thing," God replies. He is looking at me and smiling because he knows I want to hear more and want to understand better. "Be patient; we will get there. How do you feel when you try to manifest or pray for better conditions from a place of lack or needing something?"

"Well, often I'm a bit worried or fearful, or if it is something I have been wanting for a long time, I'm frustrated," I admit.

"Perfect, then all is working beautifully." He smiles.

"Perfect? How can that be perfect?"

"Think about money," God says. "How do you think you tend to pray and try to visualize to manifest more money? Is it from an inner place of knowing that all is well and abundant? And from an inner place of wholeness and completeness, therefore feeling joy of money and appreciation of money? Or do you think it is more often from a place of lack and need; therefore, feeling worry, concern or frustration?"

"Ok, I admit that I often feel worry, concern or frustration, so more often from a place of lack or need of money. But sometimes, and probably a bit more lately, I do practice feeling joy and appreciation toward money."

"So because you practice and embody two different emotional and vibrational places you experience both conditions. You have moments of doing well with money and other moments of struggle and lack of money," God says.

"Yes," I admit again.

"Currently, you really don't understand how it is that after all the studying and praying you do, you still end up manifesting the 'struggle and lack' aspect of money, thus the whining to me," He says and smiles. "You don't fully understand who and what you really are. You don't understand the vibrational nature of consciousness and how you manifest conditions in your life, and how your emotions and feelings play into this."

A great mystic tells us that the
upper part of the Soul is merged
with God and the lower part with
time and conditions.

Earnest Holmes,
The Science of Mind

God hands me two folded pieces of paper. "Here, we will leave soon and I want you to bring these with you on our trip."

"What trip?" I think to myself, but I take the papers and unfold them. Each has a different heading: "Your Inherent God Nature" is the title of one piece of paper and "Create and Manifest with God" is the other.

I glance up from the paper and look at Him. "To really answer your questions, it will help to have an understanding of each of these. They relate to each other," He explains.

I start to read the first one but hear God saying, "Just put them in your pocket for now and read them later. Think of them as tips about you and me and manifesting. Keep them; they are yours." There is a stir in the air around me. I feel an energy of sorts and start hearing the faint sound of waves.

Part 1: Your Inherent God Nature

Chapter Two

You Are an Expression of God

I feel sand under my feet. I look around, and God and I are standing barefoot on a beautiful beach. It is one of those cool and comfortable days. There is a slight breeze, a bit of cloud cover, and just the two of us. I can hear and feel silence, wind and waves like never before. I start to ask God how we got here but He begins talking to me. "Look out there and tell me what you see."

"I see waves of various sizes and they look like they go on forever."

"How many waves do you see?" God asks.

"Too many to count; there is no way I could count all of them."

"If you peered beneath the surface and into the wave and even below the wave what would you see? Would you continue to see the wave itself?"

"Umm, no I guess not; I'd see into the ocean and I'd no longer see the wave," I say.

"It is interesting how something can appear to be so individual and separate on the surface yet not be, all at the same time," God comments. "Now I want you to think about you and me. Imagine that I AM the ocean and as the ocean I desire to create and express myself as waves. I want to create and manifest life not because I need or lack anything—I am wholeness and complete; I lack nothing. I want to create simply because I love to express life, and from this sheer place of joy, love and appreciation of life, I choose to create. I choose to express myself as waves.

"So I, as the ocean, want to create waves, and from this inherent place of love, joy and appreciation for life, I express myself and waves are created. They are abundant and diverse. I have a thing for abundance and diversity if you haven't noticed," God chuckles.

I look at my feet in the sand and see an abundance of sand and how each grain is different from the other, and I see how many waves there are and how each one is unique. "Okay, I'm with you," I say.

"Now think about the waves in relationship to the ocean. Are they separate? Are they made of the same stuff? Would the ocean have awareness of the waves? Would the ocean judge the waves it has created and is now expressing itself as? Would the ocean judge the diversity and differences of the waves? If they are made of the same stuff, can the waves now create and manifest like the ocean does?"

"Well hang on, not too many questions at once; I don't want to get the answer wrong," I say.

God laughs, "No wrong answers, but I do want you to think."

"Okay, so here I go: No, it would not be possible for the ocean to ever be separate from the waves, even though the waves seem individual and separate on the surface. Yes, they definitely are made of the same stuff. Yes, it seems true that you as the ocean would always be aware of the waves you created. No, if you wanted to express yourself as a wave then it would not make any sense at all for you to turn around and judge yourself in any way. No, you would not judge the diversity and differences of the waves." I pause a moment about the last question, and then say, "Well, I guess if they are of the same stuff, then yes the wave could create and manifest in some manner like the ocean."

I want to start saying "but" and then God turns to me. It reminds me of how my grandmother used to look at me. She would give me her full attention, as if there was nothing else in the world going on except me—what an amazing feeling! God's look made me forgot about the "but" I was going to interject.

He continues, "So I want you to truly hear this but I want you to hear it with your being, not simply with your ears. I want the 'all of you' to hear me."

Okay, so if God looks directly at you in a wonderful fashion and says in His own way "Listen up!" you sort of do.

God says to me, "I am your ocean. You are my wave. I AM the source of you. Really, hear me. *I am expressing myself as you.* This is not a metaphor any more. It is truth, fact, real, here, and now.

"I am God consciousness, expressing myself as you and all things, both seen and unseen. Consciousness is alive, aware, awake, vibrational, here, now, real, present, presence. It is felt and dynamic, not static, not dead, not distant. It is here and now. I am here and now.

"You live in a world of consciousness—God consciousness. God consciousness that is both physical and nonphysical. You are physical and nonphysical consciousness, spirit and human. You are both at the same time."

I look at my hand for a moment and think about what God is telling me. This hand then is God's hand. This hand is human and spirit. God is expressing as me. I wiggle my fingers. Even though I cannot see the cells in my body right now, I realize that God is within each of them. God consciousness is making up each cell of my hand, of my body. God continues.

"There is nonphysical consciousness first, then nonphysical consciousness expressing as physical consciousness. But all of it is consciousness, and physical life as you know it to be is occurring within God consciousness." He pauses a moment to let that sink in.

We are living in consciousness and
not in conditions, so this is the way
we should look at it; there is just
life and we are in it.

Earnest Holmes, *Love & Law*

"I am your ocean; you are my wave. I AM the source of you," God continues. "This is not just philosophy, theology, quantum physics, or neuroscience. It is genuine, real and true. Your sciences are simply studying God consciousness. You still with me? You still listening with 'all of you'?" God sort of asks and states all at the same time. I simply nod because I don't want to speak. I really am listening with the "all of me."

He continues, *"You and I are not separate and can never be separate.* Separation from me is never possible, and you can never do or not do something that changes that.

"Think about anything that you have ever done and have had a hard time forgiving yourself about," God says to me. I think for a moment; it doesn't take long. "Even that," God says, "does not change what I am saying to you. I really am expressing myself as you and am always the source of you, and because I am love, joy, whole and complete, so are you."

God walks me to the edge of the water, has us both sit in the sand and let the waves wash over our feet, and continues. "Think of how wetness is a part of both the ocean and the wave. On the surface there is wetness, beneath the surface there is wetness, and at the depths of the ocean there is wetness. Wetness exists at all points in the ocean all at the same time. This is how connected to me and to others you are. Wetness everywhere, all at once and always.

"This means that God consciousness is everywhere and all at once and always."

God reaches over, splashes me with water, and laughs. "Feel that! Feel the wetness. It is the same with you and me. You can never separate me from who you are. This is true for all the billions of you alive today."

He lets a period of silence transpire as these words penetrate into me. I get a bit mesmerized as I feel the sand and water washing over my feet and I bury my toes a bit deeper into the sand. I am much more aware of the wetness of the ocean. I hear God again and feel myself refocus on His voice.

"Things get screwy when you believe we are separate. You believe things such as the feeling you are not worthy; you need to sacrifice and suffer to earn my love or receive goodness. You feel small and insignificant. You perceive that I am moody and sometimes answer prayers and other times do not. Then you think you need to pray to me a certain way and beg and plead your case to convince me to give you something. These are just to name a few. Any of this sound familiar?"

I nod yes. "All of it sounds familiar."

The Principle of Life, always active,
is ever striving to pour Itself forth
into expression, thereby producing
Its Natural Perfection; but human
beings, having free will,
consciously or unconsciously
qualify It with all kinds
of distortion

Godfré Ray King,
The I AM Discourses

"This notion of being separate from me directly relates to why you ever came to believe in lack of any

kind," God says. I hear the waves again and feel my feet in the sand as they get more grounded into it and into God.

I hear such strength in God's voice, and it seems to grow stronger. "Think deeper about this. It means that you are not a mistake; none of you are, and I did not make a mistake in creating any of you, ever. You and others often ask, what is the will of God?"

"You are the will of God; each of you is the will of God."

> *By the belief that your will is*
> *separate from mine, you are*
> *exempting yourself from the Will*
> *of God which is yourself."*

> Foundation for Inner Peace,
> *A Course in Miracles*

"So, are you worthy?" God asks.

I start to feel emotional. "Apparently immensely so," I say. I think I am feeling the truth of this and how it is true for each of us.

"I never judge you—never have, never will, can't. I am love, and that is what you get constantly, always: alive-living-love. To judge you or anyone in any way would mean I would stop being love and well-being, and I cannot do that. What happens when you judge yourself or hate yourself? Even slightly judge or hate

yourself or others? Are you still connecting to love when you do so? Can you love and judge at the same time?" God asks.

"No, uh, I guess not," I stammer.

"Does judging yourself or others inspire you or them? Motivate you or them? Bring about the change you seek?" God asks.

"No, God, it really doesn't and never has, but to be honest, doing it is quite the habit."

"And?" God says, prompting me to think further.

"And, well, even though it might be a habit, I can choose to stop myself from judging myself, hating myself or others, and choose differently. I can choose to give myself and others a break and give love instead."

"Which do you think will bring about the best results for you?" God asks.

"Well, love," I reply.

God places a hand over my heart and says, "Love is more in line with your inherent God nature, and your life will always go better when you are more in line with your inherent nature."

"God, I realize how easy it is to judge myself and how often I do so, but you're right. The moment I do it I stop allowing your love to reach me."

"Yes," God says, "in your own way you aren't allowing it, but realize that my alive-real love is still flowing to you and has not stopped."

He hands me a deep purple flower that looks exotic and tropical and smells amazing. I look around on the beach; I am not quite sure where it came from. "You like to garden, don't you?" God asks.

"Love it," I say.

"You ever get a kink in your garden hose when you are watering your plants at home?"

"Sure, more often than I would like."

"When you have a kink in the hose, is water still flowing to the kinked area?"

"Well, sure," I reply.

"When you are using your attention and focus to judge or hate yourself, others or life you create a kink, but you do not stop the love of God that is flowing to you in that moment; it is still there flowing to you. You simply disrupt your ability to receive it, to allow it.

"Pick any moment when you might hate or judge yourself, someone else, or some condition in life and in that same moment I am still sourcing love to you. Some of you have become very practiced at keeping this kink alive for months, years or even a lifetime, but all the while, love is still being sourced to you," God points out.

"At any moment, you can shift your focus and place your attention on aspects of life, yourself or the other person that you love and appreciate. The moment you start refocusing, you start opening the kink and allowing this love to reach you. When you start focusing on life, yourself, or another in this way, it aligns with your inherent God nature.

"As the source of you, your inherent nature and God's nature are the same, so that is why I said it aligns with your inherent God nature. The moment you shift your focus and begin thinking in a way that is more aligned with your inherent God nature, you will begin to experience relief. This feeling of relief means you are shifting your focus and thinking in the right direction. In a way, this is what forgiveness does for you; it helps you unkink your hose and allows you to receive the love that has always been flowing to you.

"So when I say that I source a constant, continuous, infinite stream of love to you and each of you always, not sometimes; I mean this literally. I don't do it just when I feel a certain way. I beam, source, send and pulse love to you now, now, now, and now. Like the ocean sourcing a constant stream of water to the wave. Really, know that this is not a metaphor, it is not a concept—it is the real deal. Keep listening with 'all of you'; stay with me."

God bends down to the water, cups handfuls of it and pours it back and forth between his hands and continues, "Because we are the same stuff, your essence, your inherent nature is my nature, God nature. You are birthed from, alive-living-love, joy, well-being, abundance, allness, wholeness, and completeness. This means your inherent nature, your inherent God nature, is love, is joy, is blessedness, is well-being, is abundance, is whole, is complete and lacks nothing.

"In short, *you are made of only the stuff of God*, regardless of your parents and your human experience. Nothing you have experienced or done, or that has been done to you, has ever or will ever influence, change, impact, or lessen your inherent God nature. I am not saying that because it is a nice thing to say to you; I am saying it because it is the truth.

"You do not need to earn God or earn your worth; you are it and are born with it, freely given. Your source is enlightened; therefore, your inherent nature is enlightened. You can allow it or not allow it. You are aware of it or sometimes unaware of it, but regardless, it is this way," God says.

That is, you can be conscious or
unconscious of your union with the
Divine Ground; those are the only
two choices you have.

Ken Wilbur,
The Simple Feeling of Being

"Your ability to allow, feel and experience your God nature varies to numerous degrees, like your garden hose variously has a slight kink or a major kink. But remember it can never be cut off; like wetness can never be extracted from the ocean, your God nature never stops.

"Let me repeat this piece again," God says. "There is one consciousness, God consciousness being diverse, and this one God consciousness is choosing to express as you and all others and all things. And all of this is happening in God consciousness. *I AM abundance. I AM diversity*. You are not meant to all be the same, look the same, act the same, like the same things, and believe the same ways. You hurt each other when you falsely believe this. *I am oneness being diverse*," God explains.

God is Life, not some life
but all Life.

Earnest Holmes, *The Art of Life*

"What did your dad do when you told him you were gay?" God asks. He doesn't seem to prep me before asking questions. I take a moment and think back to that experience.

"I grew up on a farm, and I remember it was just Dad and me sitting outside on the patio with a few cows by the fence. It was afternoon, and I just sort of knew this was the time to tell him. So I eventually said to him, 'Dad, I want to talk to you about something,' and paused a moment. He just looked at me and waited. 'I'm dating men,' I blurted out. Okay, it was out there now and at that point of no return. I was so frickin' nervous. Mostly afraid he would hate me and not want to see me. We have always had an easy way with each other and a closeness that I didn't want to lose.

"I remember that after the initial shock, he started sharing a lot about himself. It was as if all of a sudden someone was having a personal conversation with him, and it had been a while, so all this stuff came out. Much of what he shared was not related to this but I just listened. He talked; he got angry and, at one point, he wanted to know why I was telling him this. 'You could just live your life and not tell me about it,' he said.

"'So you don't want to know me,' I said. He paused a moment and said, 'No, that's not what I want.'

"God, emotionally it was exhausting. It felt like we talked for a long time but I remember at one point he paused and looked at me and said, 'This is different than talking about your truck like we usually do!' That made us both start laughing. But mainly I remember telling him I didn't need him to like it or agree with it, I just didn't want him treating me different. Like I said, I have always felt close and easy with him and I didn't want to lose that, and I really feared I would."

"What did he do right at the end of your conversation?" God asks.

"Well, we were wrapping up the conversation and I was getting ready to go and he grabbed my wrist. I quickly thought OH F---K!!! Here it comes, but he did not get upset. Instead, he literally pulled me onto his lap for a moment. He didn't say anything; he just held me there. He surprised me, but this was his way of letting me know that everything was okay and I never needed to worry about him treating me differently. I am pretty sure he was also saying he did not need to ever talk about it again, but he was letting me know that he and I were good. I still feel emotional when I think about how loving that was for him to do, and he never has treated me differently. And he treats Mark, my partner of 18 years and now my husband, like a son and always has."

"He chose to go with his love for you instead of fear, confusion, anger or hate," God says. "So as you look around and see all the diversity in the world, from skin colors and shapes and sizes and customs and traditions and religions and, yes, even sexual orientations, just know I pull each of you onto my lap and like your dad, send you only love."

I think God takes a breath—I know I take a few. I am aware of the sounds of the waves again; they do not look the same. There is so much more to them now than a moment ago.

For a moment, and it seems like a long moment, I simply don't know what to say or ask. And for part of that moment, I actually don't want to say or ask anything. There is something wonderful about just being with God and all I just heard. I breathe again and feel my feet in the sand.

"You remember the first time you realized in a deep way that I was real and not just a concept?" God asks.

"I do," I say. "I was reading a little book called *The Cloud of Unknowing*. As I read something in that book, I had a very visceral feeling, an experience of 'GOD IS!' It just sort of hit me in a way that had never happened before. I really *felt it* and realized you were actually real and not just a concept. I don't think I realized this before or felt it like I did in that moment. As odd as that might sound, I had always believed in you and prayed to you but had not fully known that you are real."

"It isn't that odd," God says. "I think for many I am conceptual and not truly real, or I am perceived to be a separate being. Many don't realize that everything is happening in God consciousness."

"Be still and know that I am God," I say aloud. God looks at me. "I'm just thinking about this scripture I've heard many times in my life that's always had meaning for me. 'Be Still and Know that I AM God' says a lot more than we realize. It is a truth. It is also a thing to practice and not just a nice quote," I say. "What I mean by that is there is value in just spending time in prayer and silence with you and with myself, as a way to be together and to align with you and with my inherent God nature."

"Yes," God says. "Silence is one way you refocus and shift your attention inward. You pull away or let go of the physical conditions that can be entertaining but distracting. And you let yourself be with me, your truest self, your nonphysical self and what you call your 'spiritual self' and what I am calling your inherent self and your inherent God nature. Being in silence is literally being in and with God consciousness without the distractions of physical life. Never underestimate the value this gives you."

"God, I think my Centering Prayer practice helps me with this too. I think it helps me stay connected to you and to my inherent God nature. With Centering Prayer, we don't talk and no request is being made; it is just about being together. I tend to think of it as you and me sitting on a park bench and just enjoying each other's company but not needing to speak."

"Yes" God says, "aware and just enjoying each other's presence."

> *In teaching the practice of*
> *Centering Prayer, we emphasize*
> *prayer as relationship.*
>
> Father Thomas Keating,
> *Manifesting God*

"Centering Prayer is one type of prayer that is about being with you versus the other types of prayer I use to talk with you or visualization that I use to deliberately manifest conditions in my life," I tell God. "Even when I want to talk or want to visualize better conditions in my life I still always start with Centering Prayer."

Centering Prayer is taught by Father Thomas Keating and the organization he founded called Contemplative Outreach (www.contemplativeoutreach.org).

- "Choose a sacred word as the 'symbol' of your intention to consent to God's presence and action within.

- Sitting comfortably and with eyes closed, settle briefly and silently introduce the sacred word.

- When engaged with thoughts, return ever-so-gently to the sacred word.

- At the end of the prayer period, remain in silence with eyes closed for a couple of minutes."

The recommended time for this prayer practice is 20 minutes, preferably two 20-minute periods a day. Do one first thing in the morning and another in either the afternoon or the early evening.

I simply use a timer. (I use an app called Insight Timer.) This allows me to maintain my focus and not get distracted by the time. I've been practicing Centering Prayer daily since the early 90's. Also, you can find out about Centering Prayer silent retreats through the Contemplative Outreach website. I've done 1-day, weekend, 5-

day and 10-day silent retreats as a way to continue deepening my relationship with God.

I had the pleasure of attending a lecture with Father Thomas. He is an amazing and funny man. He has written extensively on Centering Prayer and other prayers, and I recommend his readings.

"Is this practice of Centering Prayer or something similar a useful part of prayer and manifesting?" I ask.

"Yes, because it helps you embody and simply BE, and BE with who you really are. With Centering Prayer and other meditations, you continually focus on God; this continued focus allows you to constantly activate the vibration of your truest self, your inherent God nature," God says. "We will talk more about vibration in a moment.

"Before you begin things like prayer, meditation or visualizing, or you start a meeting, answer a phone call or check your emails, try centering yourself first. It is a good way to start your day or take breaks. Center first, and then proceed. Some people can do this sitting and use a practice like the one you do with Centering Prayer. Some people prefer to go on a quiet and meditative walk. Some people center by

running. Remember, I am abundant and diverse;
there isn't just one way," God says.

The directions to finding God,
which are printed on the box in
which your heart came, are simple:
relax the mind and body; with
reverence and devotion, gaze into
the Heart; feel the Love-Light
radiance that permeates your
entire body, and your entire mind,
and all of nature, and
all nations everywhere.

Ken Wilber,
The Simple Feeling of Being

God starts creating all sorts of shapes with the water.
Some are common shapes of day-to-day things and
others are simply abstract and amazing, like living art
before my eyes.

"Your God nature is designed to express, create and
manifest conditions, and it does this with or without
your awareness of it. It is inherent within you;
manifesting conditions is inherent to your being. You
simply haven't learned how to use what you are in a
deliberate way. You can create heaven on earth or
the lack of it, and you tend to do both: You think, 'I
am rich; I am poor.' Both use your inherent God
nature and can cause manifestations. How to do this

more deliberately is what we will talk about next," God says.

"I don't want you to just think upon all that I am saying and hope it's true or even just believe it. Go further into the realm of *knowing* it. I AM you, and your God nature is available to use to manifest better conditions in your life.

"I know you want to be more masterful at creating your life, so we will begin talking about this and manifesting, but first I wanted you to have a richer understanding of who you are and what you are in relationship to me; to understand how connected and one we are; to understand how loved and valued you are; and to understand how connected you are to others," God says. I look at the ocean and the waves again and feel the water and wetness against my feet in the sand.

God continues, "Alright, let's get to the stuff about you and your inherent God nature and how that relates to manifesting a better life and better conditions."

Chapter Three

The Vibrational Nature of Consciousness

God touches me on the arm; I get a shock and a vibration, and I jump a bit. He smiles and says to me, "There is a vibrational nature to consciousness that is important you understand. And there is a law woven into the fabric of consciousness, a law of your being, and this law says that conditions are drawn to match vibration.

"This is true universally and individually, meaning this law responds to your collective consciousness as a mass of people on the planet and it responds to you individually. You've come to call this law the *Law of Attraction*, but realize it is a law of consciousness, a law of your being," God explains.

"Look out there again," He says and points to the ocean. "The ocean, the waves, this beach, the air, the sky, the birds—all of it is God consciousness being expressed, all of it is occurring within God consciousness, and all of it has a vibrational nature within it."

*Consciousness is the one and only
reality. All phenomena are formed
of the same substance
vibrating at different rates.*

Neville Goddard, *Prayer:
The Art of Believing*

I look around the beach at all that God is referring to
and really think of how all of it is alive with God
consciousness and is vibrational in nature.

"God, I recall reading a wonderful book called *The
Hidden Gospel*, by Neil Douglas-Klotz. He shares that
any words Jesus would have spoken would have
been in Aramaic, and in the book, he translates
various sayings of Jesus. I found there was so much
more richness to the scriptures and sayings that I had
heard so many times before. The original Aramaic
text of 'Abwoon d'bashmaya' translates into what we
know as the opening line of the Lord's Prayer, 'Our
Father which art in Heaven.' But he explains that the
original Aramaic version can be interpreted in a
variety of ways due to the nuances of the language;
one interpretation becomes

"Father-mother who births Unity,
You vibrate life into form in each
new instant."

"And one possible translation for the second line, "hallowed be thy name," is

"All vibrating waves return to one ocean and to You, the nameless, creative one behind it."

I send a silent "thank you" to Neil to let him know his work was significant to me.

God continues, "The condition or physical life you see corresponds to a vibrational nature you do not necessarily see, and this law of consciousness, law of attraction orchestrates that. You might not see the vibrational nature of the ocean but you do see the physical manifestation of it that aligns with the vibration. You might not see the vibrational nature of you, but you do see the physical manifestation of it. You might not see the vibrational nature of your favorite chair you like to sit in but you do experience the physical manifestation of it.

"First, things are vibrational in nonphysical consciousness, and then there is a corresponding physical manifestation of it in consciousness. Both are expressions of consciousness, just different vibrational frequencies: one can be seen and one unseen. All things seen and unseen are vibrational and have a frequency."

*Everything in the universe
constantly gives off an energy
pattern of a specific frequency...*

David R. Hawkins, *Power vs. Force*

"Vibration is a language of consciousness," God says, and then gazes out toward the ocean; all becomes calm. He taps the water and a ripple goes out in all directions. "Because both physical and nonphysical consciousness are vibrational, they can be felt and experienced. You interpret, translate, and perceive vibration through your five senses of sight, smell, taste, hearing, and touch. You can see the ocean, smell it, taste it, hear it, and touch it. You experience it fully because you interpret the vibration of it through your senses. Your feelings and emotions also interpret vibration, and we will talk more about them in a moment."

God places a finger in the water and a bit of it freezes around it. "Do you remember a couple of books you read a few years ago about ice crystals and water?" He asks.

I think back, and I do remember reading a couple of small books by Masaru Emoto. *"The Hidden Messages in Water* and *The True Power of Water,"* I say.

"Tell me what you remember," God replies.

40

"What impressed me were the images of the ice crystals he studied. For example, it was amazing how he would label a jar of water with the words 'love and gratitude' and another with the words 'you fool,' and then he created ice crystals using the two jars. The ice crystals from the water with the label 'love and gratitude' on it were perfect and beautiful, and the crystals with the words 'you fool' on it were disfigured," I recall.

"The words 'love and gratitude' have a vibration and therefore a certain frequency," God says. "The words 'you fool' also have a vibration and certain frequency, and the crystals formed in alignment with the corresponding vibrations and frequencies. The law of consciousness, law of attraction matched the conditions to the vibration. In this situation, it was ice crystals. In the example you gave earlier about money, you manifest both lack of money and abundance because both vibrational frequencies of 'lack of money' and 'abundance' are active within you.

"Did the ice crystals get disfigured from the water labeled 'you fool' because the water was bad or being punished or less worthy, or because the 'God of Ice Crystals' was angry, passing judgment or in a bad mood?" God asks.

I laugh, "Well, no, of course not," I reply.

"Right. This is simply the law of consciousness or law of attraction responding to the vibrational nature of something. It is the same with you. This law is responding to you but it is not personal, though it often feels personal to you."

God touches my arm and shocks me again and laughs. "Just making sure you are paying attention." We laugh. "There are a few other things about consciousness," He says.

- "You activate the vibrational nature of consciousness by the power of your focused attention.
- Once you focus on something, whether it is the thinking going on inside your head or an external condition, you activate consciousness vibrationally.
- You think thousands of thoughts a day, but it is your focused attention to certain thoughts that activates them in consciousness.
- Based on how you perceive and think within consciousness and perceive and think about physical manifestations or life events, you tend to draw conclusions and make preferences and create beliefs.
- You then have feelings and emotions based on the conclusions, perceptions or beliefs you hold."

"So, it is not just thinking in general that activates consciousness and influences manifestations; it is focused attention on specific thoughts, intentionally or unintentionally, that activates consciousness." I say.

"Yes, you think many different thoughts throughout your day but you give more attention and focus to some thoughts and this activates them vibrationally, and law of attraction responds. We will talk about this in more detail later."

God focuses on the water again and makes more shapes like he did moments ago. I watch for a moment; they are amazingly beautiful. It really is living art. "God, you are apparently quite talented," I say lovingly and jokingly, and we laugh a bit.

"You focus, you activate consciousness, you perceive it a certain way, and then you have a feeling or emotional experience based on the way you perceived it. You think all of this is just happening in your own head, but what is going on in your head is happening in consciousness," God says.

Some may imagine that there are two worlds, one "out there" and a separate one being cognized inside the skull. But the "two worlds" model is a myth.

Nothing is perceived except the perception themselves, and nothing exists outside of consciousness.

Bob Berman & Robert Lanza, *Biocentrism*

Chapter Four

What Your Emotions and Feelings Really Mean

"Here is what your emotions and feelings really mean," God says. "You in physical form have the ability and free will to focus your attention on life and perceive it and think about it however you choose. You can think of and perceive it in ways that align with your inherent God nature, or you can think of and perceive it in ways that do not, or anywhere in between.

- "Your emotions, therefore, let you know at any moment whether you are aligned with your inherent God nature and to what degree you are allowing it.
- "You can also deliberately use your feelings· and emotions to increase your vibration when you are trying to manifest better conditions in your life."

God writes #1 and #2 in the sand. "First, a bit on how your emotions let you know whether you are aligned with your inherent God nature, and then we will chat about how to use them deliberately to manifest better conditions."

- "When you are focused on and think about something in life, about yourself or someone else, and you view it in the way your inherent God nature knows the truth of it to be, you feel your intrinsic joy, love, worth, and appreciation for life; you feel positive emotions.

- "When you think about and focus on life, yourself or another in a way that is not in alignment with what your inherent God nature knows to be true, you feel the 'offness' of it and experience negative emotions to various degrees.

- "Your emotions are not generated because of outer conditions, as you might think. Your emotions and feelings occur because of how aligned your perception or thinking is with your God nature.

- "The more aligned your perception and thinking is with your inherent God nature, the more positive the emotion. The more misaligned your perception is, the more negative your emotion."

"Therefore, you experience a full and massive range of emotions and feelings, and you experience a variety of intensity with your feelings and emotions. Your feelings and emotions let you know how aligned or misaligned you are at any given moment."

*Feeling good equals allowing the
connection; feeling bad equals not
allowing the connection-feeling
bad equals resisting the
connection to your source.*

Ester and Jerry Hicks,
Ask and It Is Given

"Let's use your situation about money that you
mentioned earlier. We were talking about how you
focus on both the abundance and the appreciation of
money but also on the lack of and struggle for it.
When you perceive or focus on lack or your financial
debt, you naturally feel worry or concern because
you are not focused on the subject of money in a
way that is aligned with your inherent God nature.
Your inherent nature knows a different truth. It
knows a truth about abundance and money and
'wholeness and completeness' and does not know a
truth of lack or debt.

"So in that moment, there is a vibrational occurrence
that your inherent God nature experiences on the
subject of your attention, money, and there is a
vibrational occurrence that you are experiencing
about the subject of your attention, money. These
are not aligned, and you feel the 'offness' of it as
worry and concern. Your feelings occur because of

the difference in these vibrations and not really because of the physical condition called money."

God looks at me, "I know, this is very different from what you think is going on, but your emotions really aren't about money and about the conditions in life. *Your emotions are about how your perception, focus, and thinking are in alignment or out of alignment with the perception of your inherent God nature in that moment.*"

God hands me a small magnifying glass. "Remember how as a kid you would gather some leaves and hold this magnifying glass above them, and as the focus of the sun was amplified by the glass it would begin to burn the leaves?"

"Sure I remember that; it was pretty cool," I say.

"Holding your focused attention on something is like holding the magnifying glass on the leaves. The longer you keep your focus on it, the more you enhance the vibration of it or activate it. The leaves can eventually catch fire. With your focused attention, your emotions and feelings will ignite to various degrees in either direction—positive or negative—depending on how aligned your thinking and your perceptions are with your inherent God nature. Think about it: if you focus on things you appreciate, you will start to feel good, because this type of thinking is aligned with your inherent God nature. Keep focusing this way and you will feel even better. When you focus on things you do not like, or you complain or hate, you will start to feel bad, because this type of thinking is not aligned with your inherent God nature; you will feel the 'offness' of it as negative emotions. If you keep focusing on it you will feel worse."

> *The time has arrived when all must understand that thought and feeling are the only and Mightiest Creative Power in Life or in the Universe. Thus the only way to the definite use of the full power of one's thought and feeling, which is God in Action, is through Self-control—Self-correction—by which one may quickly reach the attainment, the understanding whereby he may direct and use this Creative Thought-power without any limit whatsoever.*
>
> Godfré Ray King,
> *The I AM Discourses*

"You tend to let conditions in your life decide what to focus on and determine how you will feel, as opposed to deliberately deciding both," God points out.

He throws a bunch of money in the air. I look toward the sky and it just keeps falling over us. What fun!

"When you perceive or focus on the abundance of money and well-being in your own life, and the things you appreciate about money, you naturally feel better, and you feel positive emotions because you are focusing, perceiving and thinking about money in a way that aligns with your inherent God nature."

He grabs the magnifying glass again and looks through it toward me. "Your consistent focus, perception and thinking in either direction, meaning on 'abundance of money' or 'lack of money,' will magnify and intensify your emotions either positively or negatively, and the law of consciousness, law of attraction will do its thing. You said earlier that you tend to do both, you feel appreciation for money and feel worry and concern, and I said you then manifest both conditions, and you agreed, and this is why," God explains.

When you allow the attention to
become fixed upon a thing, you
that moment give it power to act
in your world.

Godfré Ray King,
The I AM Discourses

I think I start to smell popcorn, and then I see God handing me a bag of it. It is hot, salty and buttery, my favorite. We are still on the beach. I have no idea where God finds these things, but I am starting to understand a bit more. "I want to tell you a story about one of these waves" He says, and points to one of the waves. "This is a story about a wave sitting down to pay its bills." God smiles and begins telling his story. I take a bite of popcorn.

"The wave is getting ready to pay bills and is looking at its bank account and sees very little money. It sees bills, debt and lack. The wave immediately feels fear, frustration and worry and is discouraged. Now remember, these negative emotions occur because the wave is not focused on the issue of money the way its inherent God nature is. Think of these negative feelings and emotions as communication, as its inherent God nature trying to communicate to the wave.

"So the wave sits there and continues to focus on 'lack,' and the negative emotions continue and get even stronger! Yet, these negative emotions are me, God waving my God hands and saying, 'Hey, stop focusing on your finances in this way! You are viewing it incorrectly! You believe incorrectly! You are forgetting who you really are!'

"But the wave is caught up in the experience of 'lack is real' and 'money is hard' and forgetting that these negative emotions are occurring because of its current focus on this type of thinking and believing. These negative emotions are not really because of the current finances. That's the big difference.

"Can you relate?" God asks me. I nod yes with my mouth full of popcorn.

God makes a loud splash in the water. "Then it happens!" He says in a loud voice. "The wave remembers many of the teachings it has encountered over the years as it has studied. It starts to remember, 'I come from well-being, abundance, wholeness, completeness, and I can stop thinking this way. I can stop the way I'm focusing on my finances.'

"Now the wave immediately begins to refocus, rethink and reach for thoughts that are aligned with how its inner being thinks about finances. The wave begins to think about what its inherent God nature, the God within, knows about finances.

"The wave starts thinking things like 'I came from abundance so abundance does exist. I have paid my bills in the past and I will again. No one is knocking on my door to haul me away or take my house or car. Everything is actually okay. Yes, I want it better but right now it really is okay.'" God reaches for some popcorn.

"The wave takes charge of its focus and thinking and how it feels and is starting to feel a bit better. Meaning what? Is the wave's money immediately better?" God asks.

"No."

"That's right, but the wave is realigning its thinking with its source of being, source of life, its God nature, and because its thinking and focus are retuning, its emotions are changing.

"But the wave doesn't stop there," God says and splashes the water again. "The wave continues thinking similar to its God nature. The wave thinks, 'Let me appreciate this mortgage payment; it allows me to live in this house right now. Let me appreciate the money I send to pay it. Bless it, God, bless it. I come from a place of being fully blessed, I AM wholeness and complete, so let me bless this bill, bless this money, and bless the company I send it to. Let me bless all my money,' thinks the wave.

"The wave's feelings are really changing and it's feeling good now, so it keeps going. 'God, let me bless each and every penny I have ever received in my entire life and forgive me for any time I have ever cursed money and bills. I simply forgot who I really am. I am completely blessed, whole, and abundant.

This is the core of my being. So yes, bless these bills, bless this money, and let me pay this freely and joyously. Yes, joyously! Yep, let me say that one again God: let me pay this joyously! That feels really good, let me say that again, I pay this joyously!' exclaims the wave.

"So you see," God says, "the wave works its way back to alignment with its God nature, its source. Now in the midst of paying its bills it feels joy and love and appreciation. The wave recalls that its nature is blessed, so it is natural for it to bless this situation too."

God looks at me and says, "Has the amount of money changed in that moment? Nope, but the wave has returned to its God nature, its true vibrational frequency of love, joy and appreciation. The wave has shifted its consciousness, its vibrational state in consciousness."

God makes an even larger splash in the water. "And now more money can come!" He exclaims. "More money can manifest and has to manifest, especially if the wave continues to consistently interrupt itself when it receives the negative emotions, those indicators from God that let it know its focus is off! And the wave must not just interrupt the incorrect line of thought; more importantly, it must deliberately reach for the best 'God nature' thoughts it can find and shift itself emotionally. Then the wave trains itself to align with joy and love and appreciation consistently on the subject of money, so money has to manifest. It is law, law of consciousness, law of attraction; it is the law of its being," God states.

God grabs more popcorn and asks, "So now what happens the next time the wave sits down with its bills?" "Does it feel joy and appreciation and love?" I start to speak, but before I can answer, God yells out, "Heck no, that's not what happens! No, the wave gets frustrated again and starts feeling negative. So the wave's feelings are once again me trying to get its attention and saying hey! Hey! Listen up! You are doing that thing you've been practicing for 50-something years. You are focused on money in a way that is not aligned with your God nature. That's why you are frustrated. So stop it!" God splashes the water again.

"But then the wave catches itself being negative about money again, and it catches itself sooner than last time. So the wave refocuses and begins reaching for thoughts that feel better. It changes how it feels and blesses its finances again. The wave does get frustrated at first but not because it's lazy or wrong. No, the wave gets frustrated only because it has practiced a certain belief about money, so it happens quickly, like a reflex; it is on autopilot. It happens so quickly that it appears to be unconscious. But everything is consciousness, so it is simply outside of its awareness, but only at first. With practice, the wave rewires itself to align with its God nature again and again. It consistently feels joy, appreciation and love toward money, and now money is consistently abundant in the wave's life."

God completes His story about the wave paying its bills, takes the popcorn and hands me my journal.

"Remember how the other morning you woke up feeling extremely fearful and anxious, full of worry?"

"Yes," I say, "I have had quite a few mornings like that."

"But do you remember what you did to change it?"

"Yes, I deliberately sat and wrote in my journal. I searched for a thought that felt better, and then did it again and again, for about 12 minutes. I went from feeling very fearful and worried to very joyful and good. I timed it; I was curious how long it would take."

"You took charge of your focus and thinking, and your emotions and feelings followed. Not at first, but as you continued to focus and think in a way that aligned with your inherent nature your emotions caught up with it and changed. You can do this always if you choose.

"You can do it with prayer, meditation, journaling, walking, calling a friend, watching a comedy, taking a nap—anything that will help you shift your attention and refocus you in the direction of your inner being. Your emotions and feelings will let you know whether you are heading in the right direction," God reminds me.

"Is that what affirmations or positive thinking does?" I ask.

"Depends," says God. "If an affirmation or a positive statement helps you feel better, then it is working. If you say an affirmation or a positive statement, but you do not feel better, it might not be the right affirmation or statement for you. One person can say an affirmation and feel better, and someone else can say the same one and not. It is more about the shift in feeling than about the words themselves," God explains. "Also remember it's not just about your thinking. You must focus on a thought long enough to activate consciousness and let your emotions shift.

"You are practiced at following your emotions or falling victim to them instead of taking charge of them and using them to your advantage, using them to create and manifest a better life. You can always change how you feel. It can take effort but you can change how you feel."

I am about to take another bite of popcorn and God stops me. "The goal is not to always need to feel positive. I don't want you to think that there is something wrong when you feel negative emotions; there isn't. They are useful to you. I just want you to truly understand what they are about so that you can shift how you feel whenever you wish to. It may take a bit of inner work but it can be done.

"Some life events are tough on you, so don't be hard on yourself about experiencing negative emotions and even getting stuck in them. Just realize that your emotions are always letting you know in the moment how aligned or not aligned you are with your inherent God nature, and you can choose to shift how you feel by taking charge of your focus and thinking in those moments."

God puts forth an image of my mom. I catch my breath for a moment; she was so beautiful! She passed away a few years ago. "When your mom died you felt the sadness and grief and loss of her as you focused on the absence of her. She was a 'wave' like yourself, and her 'waveness' ceased to be here on earth," God says.

"And as long as you focused on the absence of her 'waveness' you felt the 'offness' of that, the sadness of it. Over time, you shifted your focus away from the absence of her to remembering her love and her laughter and fun. As your focus shifted from her absence to aspects more in line with what your God nature knows to be true, you felt better.

"Your inherent nature knows there really isn't any true death and that it is simply consciousness physical and not physical. But it was your refocusing and rethinking upon the good of her rather than the absence of her that shifted how you felt."

"God, I remember knowing that it was only her physical presence that was changed and that she was back as part of the ocean, as part of God consciousness. I knew that her spirit was and is alive and well, and simply not physical anymore. But initially that was not helpful. It didn't matter; I wanted her here in wave form, and I wanted her here with us."

"Of course you did. And don't judge yourself for that; there is no wrong in it," God says. "You are here to experience the fullness of life. You are inherent joy but this doesn't mean you are meant to feel and experience only joy. *You are joy*, so who cares if you have a bad day and experience negative emotions? Simply know that you do not have to stay in negative emotions; you do not have to live your life in them. But the goal is not a life absent of negative emotions," God says as we look at the image of my mom. I start to cry again and I know it's because I am focused on her absence.

"It seems like I stayed in a funk for about a year."

"All natural and normal," He says. "Sometimes it can take a while to shift your focus and yet all is well. But simply always know that you can."

"My focus goes back and forth even years later. I miss her laugh, love, and touch but over time it has been easier to stay focused on what I love about her and less on the absence of her."

"Your feelings and emotions really are simply ways for you to know how aligned or not aligned your current focus and thinking are to your inherent God nature. So have the experience, and then decide what you want to do from there. You want to stay sad, mad, that's fine; go for it. You want to change how you feel, go for it. Know, however, that you are not a victim of your emotions, and you can change and shift them when you want to."

God nudges me. "Remember, you have all these tips about you and me in your pocket." I pull out the piece of paper titled "Your Inherent God Nature."

Your Inherent God Nature

- God consciousness is a real thing, alive and well. God IS. I AM.

- God IS and I AM right here, right now and always.

- *Everything* physical and nonphysical is God consciousness. Everything.

- God consciousness is being expressed in infinite ways with infinite possibilities. It is one thing simply being expressed as many things at the same time. "I AM this and I AM that and I AM here and I AM there."

- You are God consciousness being expressed in physical form; therefore, you are an expression of me. I AM you. All of you are.

- No separation between you and God exists.

- You are two things at the same time. You are nonphysical God consciousness and you are physical form expressed in God consciousness. Spirit and human occurring in God consciousness.

- You are not alive and then dead; you are simply alive in physical form and then alive in nonphysical form. Aliveness continues...form changes.

- Right now, in this very moment, the part of you that is in nonphysical consciousness, your inherent God nature, is literally joy, love and well-being. Whole and complete. You lack nothing. Your life experiences do not change this, ever.

- Your inherent nature is God nature. We are the same stuff.

- God consciousness, in nonphysical form and in physical form, exists at different vibrations or frequencies, but it is still God consciousness.

- You can read or perceive vibration through all of your senses (sight, smell, sound, touch, taste) *and* through your emotions and feelings.

- Your "spirit" or "inherent God nature" (nonphysical) has a vibration/frequency. Your physical you has a vibration/frequency.

- Your emotions and feelings are how you experience your alignment with your highest self, your God nature.

- You can feel when you are aligned with your God nature and also feel the "offness" of it.

- Love has a vibration/frequency. Hate has a vibration/frequency.

- When you focus on and think about something in life and view it the way your highest self knows the truth of it to be you feel good, positive emotions.

- When you focus on and think about life in a way that is not in alignment with what your highest self knows to be true you feel the "offness" of it. The frequency or vibration of your current focus in that moment is not in alignment with the frequency and vibration of your God nature and you feel this "offness," which registers as negative emotions.

- There is a law of consciousness, a law of attraction, responding to the vibrational nature of you.

Part 2: Create and Manifest with God

Chapter Five

Manifesting by Blessing Life

I smell the ocean again and sneeze. "God bless you," God says and smiles. He points to the #2 that was drawn in the sand, which was about using my emotions to deliberately manifest better conditions. "Let's start generally and then get specific about how to use your inherent God nature to manifest better conditions in your life. Let's start with just thinking about blessing or cursing life."

There is another moment of silence. I tune in to hearing the waves, and then there is a slight breeze again. I can't help but realize now that the air around me is also God consciousness made manifest. Huh, so you really can breathe God in.

"Close your eyes," God says. I snap out of my moment.

"What?"

"Close your eyes," God repeats. All of a sudden, the silence is energized, not turbulent or scary, but energized, excited in a way, and I feel a bit disoriented. "Open your eyes." I open them, and we are looking out at hundreds of people on a busy city street. "Look out there and tell me what you see," says God. I take a deep breath and get my bearings.

"I see lots and lots of people going in all different directions," I say.

"How many?" God asks.

"Well, way too many too count, but hundreds for sure," I say.

"So based on what we just experienced together on the beach, what do you really see?" God asks.

Uhumm...another God quiz. "At first glance I see a bunch of people going about their business. A bunch of individuals."

"And," God asks, "what are they really?" I think for a moment.

"They are you, God consciousness being expressed in a huge number of various ways." I say this, and then I really let myself see. A true "OMG" moment. These really are expressions of God, each one of them in all their differences. Then I remember there are billions of us and not just the few hundred I see in front of me.

"That's right," God says, "I told you I have a thing for abundance and diversity. So when you bless them or curse them, what are you actually blessing and cursing?" He asks.

"What?" I say, not sure at first how to answer. Then I repeat the question: "When I bless someone or curse someone what actually happens? Jeeezz. Okay, relax and think," I say to myself, and I remind myself that there are no wrong answers; God just wants me to actually think.

"By bless," God says, "I mean you are offering love and well-being, thinking and wanting the best for them or you or life. Cursing, meaning you are offering hate or judgment, complaining or griping about them, you or life."

So I think about how blessing someone, or even myself, would be activating something good in the ocean, in consciousness. But it hits me. Blessing not just a portion of consciousness, but all consciousness. Blessing someone is automatically reaching them in consciousness (wetness is everywhere at the same time). Because we are all of the same God stuff, in a way I am blessing myself, too. Then I realize that when I curse or judge someone or myself, I am cursing them and cursing myself at the same time. I share my thoughts with God.

"What you give you receive," God says, "*There is only one consciousness to give to and receive from.*

"I know you have heard that most of your life, but I want you to have a better understanding of why it is that you receive what you give. Whether it is positive or negative, whether you offer love or hate, whether you bless life or curse it, you are doing so in consciousness. It has a vibrational nature, and there is a law of consciousness, law of attraction responding to it. You do have free will, but that does not change the laws of how God consciousness works." I start thinking about how praying for others and distant healing really can work. All is consciousness.

> *To realize that we vibrated into form, that a sense of divine guidance influences our lives, is indeed a marvel. To consider the other side of the equation, that our individual lives may affect the whole stream of existence, boggles the mind.*

> Neil Douglas-Kloz,
> *The Hidden Gospel*

"Remember your worst boss, whom you hated?" God asks.

"Sure, it's easy to remember him; it was an awful experience."

"Remember how you were filled with anger and hatred for a while, and you literally began to feel it having an effect on you?" God asks.

"I do remember feeling as though continuing to be angry and hating him was toxic for me. For months, I constantly had fights with him in my head."

"I want you to think about what you did to change that."

"Well, I remember I was reading this great book called *My Grandfather's Blessings* by Rachel Naomi Remen, and it inspired me to begin to bless him each and every time I thought of him. I did this literally each time," I tell God.

"I remember journaling often, and other times just blessing him in my head. Literally, anytime the anger and hate would build up I'd stop myself and picture him, and wish for him all the good things I wished for myself. I remember too that I worked to genuinely feel this from my heart and to want these things for him. I tried to feel it and not just say the words."

"And as you shifted your focus and thinking to something that was more in alignment with your inherent nature, do you remember what that did?" God asks.

"I do; I remember that I began to genuinely feel a bit less anger and hate and actually shifted to a place where I really did want good things for him. It didn't feel like that at first, but it did shift to that."

"And what I really remember" I say, excited again, "is that after doing this for about two weeks I got a brand new boss whom I loved, and that was absolutely fantastic, a miracle really!"

"Perfect," God says. "You initially got caught up in the negative life experience you were having. You had your focus set on all the reasons you hated the guy, so your emotions were negative and intense because your focus was very much not aligned with your inherent God nature, which does not hate. You were set on anger and hate for quite a while. By law of consciousness, law of attraction, more conditions that were negative continued. Do you recall that?"

"Yes; I kept having more negative experiences and bad interactions with him. It was pretty awful."

God continues, "But when you deliberately shifted to thinking and seeing yourself giving love, good, and blessings to him you were shifting your focus to be in alignment with the God within you. You in turn felt better. You deliberately shifted your consciousness and vibrational state and, by law, you received love, good, and a blessing in the form of a new and improved boss.

"When we began, I said you are always dealing with consciousness and not conditions. By deliberately changing your thinking and consciousness about your boss by blessing him, you shifted how you felt; you shifted your vibration, and the law of consciousness, law of attraction shifted the condition for you. You did all of that by deciding to shift your focus and attention and thinking. *Shift consciousness, and the conditions will take care of themselves because of the law of consciousness, law of attraction.*"

> *Do you not see that in this Consciousness, there is no other Presence to act, except what you are conscious of?*
>
> Godfré Ray King,
> *The I AM Discourses*

"So when I was focused on everything I disliked about my boss and his actions I felt anger and hate, negative emotions, because this focus was not aligned with what my inherent God nature knows to be true. Is that correct?" I ask.

"Yes; your focus was on all things you did not like or want, and the 'offness' of this registered as negative emotions," God replies.

"And then when I began to shift my focus and bless him and want only good for him this was more aligned with my inherent God nature, and therefore I began to feel relief and better and more positive emotions."

"Exactly," God says. "And of course the law of consciousness, law of attraction responded to both, its law."

"Thy will be done on earth as it is in heaven," I say to God.

He smiles and looks at me. "What about it?"

"It is a part of scripture, a quote I have heard throughout my life. If I think of 'heaven' as pure God consciousness and us as being expressions of you then there is already heaven on earth. We, as people and nature, are heaven on earth. The dramas in life are simply us distorting heaven on earth, but when we bless life, self or others and do so more and more instead of cursing it or complaining, we allow more and more of heaven on earth.

"In the book I referred to earlier, *The Hidden Gospel*, Neil Douglas-Klotz offered a few translations of 'Thy will be done on earth as it is in heaven.' I find them fitting with all you have been sharing with me:"

"Let your delight flow
through us, in wave and
particle."

"Let your pleasure
manifest in us, in light and
form."

"Each of you has more influence in life than you realize just by blessing life," God says.

"Let's be clear about something, though. When you were cursing your boss, you were defiantly impacting yourself in a negative way, but never were you harming your inherent God nature of love, good, joy, peace, abundance, well-being. Never," God says.

"Well that's good news," I say. "It's very hard to constantly bless life and not get caught up in it and react to it in negative ways at times."

"Love vibrates at a much higher frequency than your hatred," God says.

"So all the times that I or others offer negativity to the world or ourselves, it's never impacting this inherent place of love, good, well-being and joy?" I ask.

"No; regardless of how long the negativity occurs, it will always exist at a different vibration/frequency than your God nature and can never cause harm to it, lessen it, impact it or touch it," God explains.

There is a slight stir in the air. God brings me back to the beach, walks us over to a large open section, and hands me a stick. "Place a very small dot in the sand anywhere," He says. I take the stick and put the smallest dot in the sand that I can make. "Excellent. Let's say that dot represents the negativity generated by the misuse of your inherent nature. Everything else around you, the entire rest of the beach, ocean, and sky, represents the amount of well-being that exists at the same time, now and always."

I let my eyes focus down the beach as far as I can see, I glance out at the ocean and up toward the sky, and then I glance down at my little dot. "The amount of well-being is and will always be huge in comparison," God says. "You and others, and most of the news you listen to, tend to focus on this small dot of drama. It is entertaining and does really grab your focus and attention, BUT" He says in a louder voice, "all is well and all is always well, regardless of what you choose to focus on and deem as real."

"God, I don't know that I can continuously bless life. Stuff happens and it gets to me, and I do at times get caught up in the drama of it," I say.

"No worries; it's not a requirement, but realize that it does make a difference in your life."

God takes the stick and points it in the sand. Then He moves it and points it elsewhere in the sand. He does this a few times, and I stay focused on the stick as it moves around. "You simply are not as practiced at controlling your focus and attention and turning toward well-being. You have practiced letting life conditions determine where you will focus, just as your eyes right now are following this stick and you have practiced turning toward negativity. But it really takes practice," God says.

"Like you did with your boss, you can deliberately change how you focus and think within consciousness, and therefore change how you feel and thus change your vibrational state within consciousness. This will always change your conditions. It simply takes practice. Remember, I said you are always dealing with consciousness and not with conditions," God reminds me.

"You tend to journal and use Centering Prayer to train yourself to focus better. But you can watch a comedy and laugh, call a friend, or go for a walk—there are endless ways to shift your focus and attention. But you have to decide to do it when needed," God says. "But remember, the time you focus on drama and feel negative never harms or impacts your inherent nature."

*I wish the students to understand
that the Stream of Life flowing
through the mind and body always
comes into them pure and
unadulterated, containing within it
all the strength, courage, energy
and wisdom that can ever be
desired; but by the lack of control*

of their thought and feeling, they are unknowingly requalifying this Pure Essence with the outer ideas upon which the attention has been fixed.

Godfré Ray King,
The I AM Discourses

Chapter Six

Manifesting with God on Purpose

"Ok, here's a joke for you," God says. "Why can't you trust God consciousness?" I shrug. "Because it makes up everything! Get it...it makes up everything?" I laugh.

"I have somewhere else I want to take you, and then we can get into more specifics about using your inherent God nature and your emotions to manifest specific conditions," God says.

"But before we talk about using your inherent God nature to manifest something specific in your life, remember that a general way to manifest better conditions is to deliberately focus, bless life and appreciate aspects of your life that you love, from little things to big things. All of it is consciousness, and the conscious act of blessing and appreciating aligns with your inherent God nature and shifts you vibrationally. By law, this attracts better life conditions and they keep coming your way."

"If it is money you want, then bless it and appreciate it. If it is a better job, then bless it and appreciate it. If it is more business, then bless it and appreciate it.

If it is a better relationship, then bless it and appreciate it. Bless it, meaning genuinely, within your heart, see the good, feel the good, want the good, give the good, see the best of the situation or the person. Pay attention to how you feel because your emotions and feelings are your guide. And do it repeatedly, not just once."

I find myself standing in a car lot. No beach, no city— it is an actual car lot, of all places. No closing my eyes this time; we just are there. "Okay, let's talk specifics about how to create and manifest with God and what happens when you desire something or pray for something and you also want to use your inherent God nature to deliberately manifest better conditions," God says. I reach into my pocket and touch the piece of paper with that title.

"Earlier I mentioned that I create by knowing and from a place of wholeness and completeness. So think about what it means to you to truly 'know' something. Not hope, not believe, not wish, but actually KNOW it to be true, a fact of your life. What does that mean to you?" God asks.

"Well, knowing means it is like a fact. It is tangible. It is done and here and now and a fact. I can feel it, touch it, interact with it," I reply.

"Yes. It is a fact and real. And when you receive something you really want, how do you tend to feel about it?" God asks.

"Well, excited, happy, joyful, blessed, full of appreciation."

"When you desire something like friends, a better job, more business, a relationship, a car, money, more love, a new home, better health, whatever it is, *your God nature receives your requests and in consciousness, vibrationally, you with your request becomes done.*" I mean this; in consciousness, this version of you becomes literally done. Let that sink in," God says.

"This means that you with the better job, you with more business, you with the better relationship or you with more money is received and now complete and known in consciousness and therefore vibrationally exists."

God walks me over to an empty spot in the car lot. I look around, look at God, and wait. Before me, a mist of sorts appears, and the image of a car becomes visible. It has a shimmer to it and I hear a faint hum. It is a car but not actually solid; it is still in a type of mist state. I peer into the windshield and see someone. It looks like me! Me sitting behind the steering wheel! "Go ahead and touch the car, I know you want to," God says. He is right; I am a bit fascinated and do want to touch it. I reach out to feel the hood of the car but can't. It is there and I can see it as a mist but I can't actually touch anything. I wave to myself and my mist-self waves back.

"Not being able to touch it doesn't mean it's not real. Your desire is vibrationally real in consciousness, but it is not just your desire that is real vibrationally.

"It is you with your desire that is real in consciousness. You with your desire fulfilled exists now within your inherent God nature.

"The version of yourself with the car simply has not fully manifested itself physically as a condition in your life, but it can if you allow it to," God says. The mist and the car with me in it vanish.

"The version of you in consciousness went from you without the new car, without the better job, without business, without the improved finances to a version of you with the new car, with the better job, with more business, with improved finances. This occurred once you began to genuinely desire this better version of yourself. After you genuinely desired it, in consciousness, you then existed with your desire fulfilled, done, KNOWN, WHOLE AND COMPLETE. And this new space in consciousness of you with your desire complete has a vibration to it that is different from the version of you without the desire complete," God says.

"So remember, your inner work is to shift *your consciousness*, not a condition. To shift it to include a concept of you, a version of you with your desire fulfilled just as your inherent God nature has done. Your inner work is to become a vibrational match with your inherent God nature about this desire, this prayer request. Once this is sufficiently done, by law the condition will manifest. This is why I say you are dealing with consciousness and not with conditions.

"Your job is to deliberately focus in a way that allows you to also 'know' the doneness of it in your own consciousness. To see it, feel it, touch it, play with it, smell it, hear it, lick it, emotionally experience it, hear you tell a friend about it, and really KNOW the doneness of it. Know it to be a fact in real, present time.

"As you do this, you will feel the positive emotions that let you know that you are focusing on your desire the same way your inherent God nature is focused on your desire.

"You do not 'want' the relationship; you are in the relationship. You do not 'want' the better job; you are working in the better job. You do not 'want' more business, you are experiencing more business," God explains. "This is a subtle difference but vibrationally different and important. The law of consciousness, law of attraction is precise. If you vibrationally 'want' you will get conditions leading to more 'wanting.'"

I look at the space where the mist of a car used to be. "You are doing fine; keep doing your best to understand these things," God encourages me.

- "The version of you being held within your inherent God nature is always whole and complete, it is not a version of you wanting or lacking anything, ever!
- "You are dealing with consciousness and not conditions. You are shifting consciousness, not conditions.
- "You must shift *your own* consciousness, the *concept of you*, to now align with the consciousness within your own inherent God nature. To shift to a living concept and a consciousness of you with your desire fulfilled.
- "Shift consciousness, shift your consciousness, and the conditions will take care of themselves. That is law: the law of consciousness, the law of attraction. The law of your own being."

Be still and know that you are that
which you desire to be, and you
will never have to search for it.

Neville Goddard,
The Power of Awareness

"Use your prayer time, your visualization time, to convince yourself of this new version of you. I do not need convincing." God looks at me. I smile.

"Guilty," I say. "I have often thought I needed to convince you, to plead my case to you for you to give me what I wanted."

"Your inherent God nature does not need convincing. From the perspective of your inherent God nature, it is already done, whole, complete and known," God says.

"Is there a best way for me to shift my consciousness, my concept of myself, to convince myself, to fully accept that my desire is truly done and real?" I ask.

"I am abundant and diverse," God says. "There are multiple ways. Remember that your feelings will let you know if what you are attempting is helping you align with your inherent God nature. What has worked for you in the past?"

"I've done meditations, journaling, journaling that includes images and pictures to help me visualize my desire done. These days, I tend to first use Centering Prayer to get quiet and aligned with you, with my inherent God nature, and then I begin to visualize me with my desire complete and done. I do my best to picture it complete. I visualize me interacting with it, having fun with it, talking to someone about it. I do work to pay attention to how I feel and reach for thoughts and images that cause me to have feelings of joy, appreciation about the desire. I will genuinely do this to feel it as a now, real thing in my life. And as I do this I do actually start feeling the fun, joy and appreciation of the desire. I feel different after.

"A while back, I read a book called *Zero Limits* by Joe Vitale about a Hawaiian healing process called Ho'oponopono. I also attended a Ho'oponopono workshop. The workshop was interesting but the main thing I learned was the power of using four phrases: 'I love you,' 'I'm sorry,' 'forgive me' and 'thank you.' I have had experiences where this has also helped me shift my consciousness, feel better and improve conditions.

"To me, using these phrases works because they all help me align with my inherent God nature in a similar way that blessing life does. When using these four phrases I am in a sense blessing consciousness, the one consciousness that is God consciousness. As I repeat them with feeling, I find I start feeling better about the situation or condition I focus on while saying the four phrases.

"I recall a two-day meeting I was participating in. Day one was challenging, and there were a couple of strong personalities in the room, including my own! So, after the meeting and in the evening I thought about all of us, and then recited the four phrases repeatedly. I did it until I felt better, until I had an emotional shift. I then continued to do it throughout the evening. Day two was amazing, and better than I could have imagined or figured out on my own," I say.

"Your use of stillness, focus, thinking, visualizing, or the four phrases all align with your inherent God nature. And the important part is that you use them until you feel different and better. You really are shifting your consciousness to be aligned with your inherent God nature, and your emotions are letting you know this," God says.

"Remember, the techniques available to you are many and varied but your goal is to shift your consciousness, shift yourself emotionally and vibrationally, so that you align with your inherent God nature and allow it to flow. Do it repeatedly and consistently so that you embody this place emotionally and therefore vibrationally. Embody it so deeply that even the cells and nerves of your body believe you," God states. "Your neurology will shift accordingly."

I can literally feel energy in the air around us. "As you practice your techniques and shift consciousness and shift how you feel, the only thing missing at this point is the physical manifestation. But rest assured that your request has manifested in nonphysical consciousness; it has manifested vibrationally," God adds. "And the law of consciousness, the law of attraction, is responding."

When you change your energy,
you lift matter to a new mind, and
your body vibrates at a faster
frequency.

Dr. Joe Dispenza,
You Are the Placebo

All of a sudden, we are in a neighborhood with only three houses on the street. Each house has a front porch with white posts. Instead of house numbers appearing on a post to identify each house, a different word is painted on a post. One house has HOPE painted on it, one house has BELIEF painted on it, and the third has KNOW painted on it. "Seeing is not believing," God says. "Hoping is not believing, and believing is not knowing. But HOPE does live right next door to BELIEF and belief lives right next door to KNOWING.

"Repeatedly focusing on specific thoughts with feelings and emotions leads to believing. Continue this over time and you come to KNOW. Spend time deliberately feeling the joy, love and appreciation of the creation itself. Bring yourself to an inner place of knowing it is done. This is what your inherent God nature, your inner being knows, so now you need to join in and align with it," God says.

> *Therefore I tell you, whatever you ask for in prayer, believe that you have received it, and it will be yours.*
>
> Mark 11:24

"Walk with me over here," God says. As we walk in front of the houses, the scene shifts and suddenly He is walking me through the car lot again. We head over to an old midnight blue Toyota 4Runner, one of the first types they ever made with a hard top that could be unbolted and removed. "Was manifesting this car easy for you or difficult?" God asks.

"What? Is this really my first car? Wow!" I reach over and touch the car. It is real this time. I look through the window. It is definitely used but it is the same car.

"It was actually easy and fun," I reply.

"Tell me about it," God requests.

"Well, it was during a time in my life when our relationship was shifting."

"Shifting how?" God asks.

"I grew up with a version of you that was about the church, and then in college I had a great experience with the Catholic student center and you became more personal to me. Jesus became personal and real to me also. At one point, I even considered being a priest, but for different reasons chose not to. I was finding I was passionate about spirituality but not about religion. I really wanted a deeper understanding and a deeper relationship but there was still very much a separate you and a separate me. I really struggled with you, and I remember sort of 'firing' you." I laugh. "The version of you I had come to know wasn't enough."

"Go on," God encourages.

"Well, as life went on I ended up moving to San Antonio for grad school and then to the small town of Victoria, Texas. It was there I met folks who introduced me to the book *A Course in Miracles*, and they had a study group that I joined. I also started listening to tapes by Jack Boland, a Unity minister, about visualizing. I started studying books by Earnest Holmes, such as *The Science of Mind* and many others. I also remember reading *The Way of a Peaceful Warrior* by Dan Millman. All of this was so different from what I had been learning but it all felt right to me, and my relationship with you got stronger. I used visualizing as a form of prayer to manifest this 4Runner."

"What did you actually do?" God asks.

"Well, every day I would sit in my bedroom and get quiet and prayerful. Then I would visualize myself driving this car, and I could even smell it. I would feel the texture of the cloth on the seats and the steering wheel. I remember feeling the fun and joy of owning the car and going camping and doing things in it. I definitely wanted one that was midnight blue, too."

The attention is the channel by
which God's Mighty Energy,
through thought and feeling, flows
to its directed accomplishment.

Godfré Ray King,
The I AM Discourses

"The Toyota dealer in Victoria had one exactly like I wanted, the right color and everything, but I thought it was too expensive. But I kept visualizing and feeling the fun and joy of it and going about my day-to-day life.

"I remember driving through Houston, Texas and thinking I might find a better price on a new 4Runner there because it was a larger city. So I checked out a few dealers. They were cheaper than the one in Victoria, but none of them had one that was the midnight blue color I wanted. One of the dealers checked his computer system to see who else might have a midnight blue one. As he checked he looked at me and said that there was only one midnight blue one in the entire state of Texas, which by the way is a pretty big state. And amazingly enough, it was in the town of Victoria!" I exclaimed.

"So I made my way back to Victoria, and I kept visualizing and feeling the joy and fun of owning this midnight blue 4Runner. The Victoria dealer called me to see if I still had any interest in it. I told him about my trip to Houston and how their prices were much cheaper. He invited me in and matched their price, and I was able to buy that midnight blue 4Runner, the only one available in the entire state of Texas!"

"How did that make you feel?" God asks.

"Well, amazing, just amazing. It was like I really was a part of the universe and not separate. It was more meaningful than just getting the car," I say.

"That's perfect," God says.

"This experience is different than what you did to receive a new boss. In this situation you desired something specific and used your inherent God nature, prayer and visualization to help bring it about, which shifted your consciousness, vibration, emotions and therefore the condition. But with your boss, you weren't trying to deliberately manifest something new; you simply knew you needed to feel better. So you simply blessed the situation in a very real, genuine and heartfelt way, which shifted your consciousness, vibration, emotions and therefore the condition," God explains.

I reach into my pocket and pull out the second paper, titled "Create and Manifest with God." God glances over. "Yep, that is what you did. You deliberately created and manifested with God." I glance over the paper as a reminder of what God has taught me.

Create and Manifest with God

- Make a request.

- God consciousness receives your request. In consciousness, your request becomes vibrationally done, whole and complete and known.

- This version of you, this version of consciousness— you with your desire done—now exists within your inherent God nature. It exists within God consciousness.

- Use prayer to quiet yourself, to focus yourself and align with your inherent God nature before you visualize.

Use visualizing and focused imagining to bring in your senses of touch, smell, sight, hearing and feelings. This helps you experience your desire as complete, whole and real, which helps you shift from not just believing but to an inner place of knowing.

- Do this deliberately to reach a point of feeling and knowing the doneness of your desire as a fact of your life. Don't simply treat these teachings as a concept; genuinely apply them until you consistently change how you feel. Practice, and train yourself to accept and KNOW it is real, done, and factual, even though you do not have physical manifestation yet.

- Consistently ignite your consciousness with thoughts and feelings of joy, love and appreciation. Deliberately enhance your vibration to match that of your inner being.

- Do this consistently, daily, not just once or twice. This allows you to embody the realness of it and the felt experience of it, so you can shift your consciousness, your concept of yourself. Again, go beyond it being a conceptual game; align with the realness and truth of it and change how you feel. A lack of consistency relates to why you sometimes do not manifest conditions you want. Use visualization to shift your concept of yourself, your consciousness, and bring yourself to a place of knowing and feeling it is done. This inner vibrational place is significant, not the technique you use.

- Do not lose your focus or begin to focus on negative beliefs, such as "I don't deserve it" or "this won't happen" or "my well-being or survival depends on this." Because this type of thinking and believing does not align with your inherent God nature, it leads to negative feelings, such as doubt, worry, fear and frustration. This also relates to why you sometimes do not manifest conditions you want.

- Create for fun!

- Visualizing to force the manifestation or trying to will it into being or to "make it happen" is vibrationally different than coming from a place of "knowing it is yours and done" and feeling joy and confidence in its arrival.

- Simply enjoy yourself and the process. In short, get out of the way and allow things to happen. Trying to force it, or will it into being and "make it happen" also relates to why you sometimes do not manifest conditions you want.

- Ultimately, shift your consciousness and deliberately use your emotions, and therefore shift your vibration. Fully accept this new concept, this new consciousness of yourself with your desire fulfilled, and the law of consciousness, law of attraction, law of your being will arrange it to manifest for you.

"That is true God; as I think upon that experience, I recall how I easily just felt the fun and joy of the 4Runner—I really wasn't trying to force it and make it happen. That lines up with what you were saying. I was teaching myself to know the 4Runner as mine and *felt* it to be a fact. I also was generating the feelings of joy and appreciation and coming from a place of wholeness and completeness, not lack or need or worry. Then by what seemed like magic the conditions aligned and the car manifested."

"Yes, it does seem like magic. You shifted consciousness. You became a new version of consciousness with you and your new car and brought it to life literally. And by law, it was arranged," God says.

He changes the subject. "What happens lately when you think about your great nephews and nieces?"

"Honestly, I tend to feel bad. I travel a lot, and I don't feel like I spend enough time with them and play with them. I worry about not having a good relationship with them."

"Perfect," God says.

"Well, it doesn't feel perfect."

"Sure, but it is a good example. Your focus and thinking in that moment are on the lack of spending time with them; they are on what you do not want. This creates a certain vibration/frequency within you. At the same time your inherent God nature knows what you do want: you want to play with them. Now this place, the space of you and your nephews and nieces playing together, exists in consciousness, complete, whole and done and known. Therefore, it exists vibrationally. As I said when we started, I create by knowing. So your inherent God nature, consciousness, knows the 'doneness' of what you want, and this has a certain frequency and vibration.

"You said you feel bad when you think about them, and that's because your focus is on what you don't want; therefore, it's not aligned with what your inherent God nature knows to be true about this subject or issue," God says.

"What happens if you start thinking about your love for them, imagine playing with them and hearing their laughter and seeing them run around your home?"

"Well, when I think about it I feel better; I feel the joy of it all," I say.

"Exactly," God says. "When you shift your thinking and focus toward what you want, your focus aligns with what your inherent God nature knows to be true and done about the issue. Your improved feelings of joy and love are letting you know that you are shifting your focus and thinking in the right direction. So your work now is to simply notice when you feel bad, and then shift your focus. Repeatedly shift your focus until you feel better. Keep doing it so that it becomes natural to you. Guess what will happen?"

"I will end up spending more time with them and having fun."

"Yep, that is what will happen," God says.

Soon after writing this piece about wanting to spend more time with my great nieces and nephews, several things occurred. As I was visiting my dad, two of my great nephews showed up unexpectedly, and I was able to visit with them. A week later my niece, the mother of two of my great nieces, called and arranged to meet me at a festival, so I got to hang out and play with them. Other moments like these have continued to occur.

"God, I don't mean to sound unappreciative, but can we talk about why it doesn't seem to work for me with some things? I have actually done this with my vehicles over the years and it works great each time. Even my current Subaru worked out perfectly, but with other subjects like money I struggle."

God tells me to hand him a $50 bill.

"I don't have a $50 bill," I say.

"Sure you do, reach into your left front pocket." I reach into my left front pocket and pull out a $50 bill. "You've said that money sometimes works and other times it's a struggle."

"Yes, well besides this very moment of pulling $50 out of my pocket, often it is a struggle," I laugh. "It is better, but difficult."

"Let's look at some reasons why it might be difficult, unlike a car. Didn't you even win a car?" God asks.

"Yeah, I forgot about that. I was traveling in Bahrain and bought a raffle ticket for a Jaguar sports car. Months later, I got a call early in the morning telling me I had won it. I had a moment of panic because I had forgotten about the ticket and was not exactly sure where I had put it. But I found it and won the car."

"So why do you think you are able to manifest a car consistently but not money?" God asks.

"I'm not really sure," I say, "but you mentioned some things a moment ago that caught my attention. You mentioned not being consistent, having negative beliefs, and trying to make it happen. As I think about those three things I think I do all of them when it comes to money but not to cars. It is just easier to feel myself owning a car than being financially free," I admit.

God claps his hands and I hear a loud roar of thunder in the sky. Now that he has my full attention, he continues.

Chapter Seven

Three Reasons Why We Don't Manifest What We Want

Reason One

"Being consistent matters. You can't manifest abundance consistently if you feel joy and appreciation sometimes but then keep going back to focusing on debt and feeling negative, worried and fearful," God says.

> *Just changing your beliefs and*
> *perceptions once isn't enough. You*
> *have to reinforce that change*
> *over and over.*
>
> Dr. Joe Dispenza,
> *You Are the Placebo*

"You can be vibrationally and emotionally consistent when you can keep your focus consistent. Meaning, when you can keep yourself vibrationally focused on what you want," God says.

"It is like with your boss; you were committed to changing how you thought and how you felt, and therefore you were consistent and diligent in your efforts. Throughout each day, you stopped yourself when you noticed you were arguing with him in your head and feeling anger and hate. You stopped yourself and refocused on blessing him. But you were consistent. This consistency is what helped you embody new thinking, a new emotional and vibrational place in consciousness.

"If you had not been consistent you would not have truly shifted your own consciousness or how you felt, nor would you have shifted your vibration enough to make a difference. The law of consciousness, law of attraction would have brought you more of the same conditions to match your vibration. In other words, you would have continued to have bad experiences with your boss or other bosses and started to feel stuck in your life. This is what happened initially and why it went on for the period of time it did, until you decided to deliberately feel better about it and began blessing him.

"You consistently shifted your focus and your feelings and got a new boss. You were consistent in imagining and feeling the car as yours and feeling the joy of it, and you received the car."

God opens the door to the 4Runner and tells me to get in. As we sit there, the radio comes on. "Hit the scan button," He says. I hit the button and the radio starts to scan stations. Rock, country, pop—each station plays a moment then moves on to another. "Being inconsistent is similar to constantly changing stations," God says. "You send out different vibrational frequencies, all of which the law of consciousness, law of attraction respond to.

"Sometimes, you use your focus deliberately and visualize deliberately and start to feel really good, like you did when you visualized this 4Runner. But with money, you begin well and start to feel good but then shift your focus and start focusing on the debt again, or the lack of money, and you start feeling worry and concern again. It's like tuning in to one station called Abundance then switching to another station called Lack. You lose your consistency and do not maintain your vibrational focus."

If your mind is scattered, it is quite powerless. Distractions here and there open the way for counterproductive emotions.

His Holiness the Dalai Lama, *How to See YOURSELF As You Really Are*

"With vehicles, you appear to maintain your vibrational focus and have an easier time of it. You keep yourself on the same 'station.' *You keep yourself vibrationally and emotionally focused,*" God says. "Have you easily manifested other things beside cars?"

I think for a moment. "Careers. Years ago, I started a private practice as a therapist, but I also missed doing physical work and started a small landscaping business. I did both part time. I used prayer and visualizing and both manifested. Many years later, I decided I wanted to take a break from being a therapist and go into consulting and training as a profession. So I used prayer and visualizing to manifest that job. I remember that I made a list for you with aspects of the career I wanted, which included international travel. I ended up getting a job as a consultant and trainer with an international company that included international travel. To date, I've been to about 30 countries.

"Even our current house was a home I used to walk by with our dogs. I just loved it. I would picture us living there and having fun, enjoying the porches and gardens. Then one day I was walking my dogs and a friend tells me that the person who owned the house wanted to sell it. That was about the same time I won the car we talked about earlier. I sold the sports car, which gave us the money to help buy the house.

"I also used visualizing to sell the home we were living in. I remember having a picture of it with a sold sign on it in my journal, and I thought it would be fun if whoever bought it paid cash. And that is how it all worked out: The person who bought it ended up paying cash for it.

"I have also had many day-to-day things work out well: traffic conditions, scheduling things, the timing of calling someone, and many more. I travel a lot, and even when the odds for a flight working out well do not look good, things usually turn out okay. I often inwardly focus on reminding myself that things work out often, and I do so consistently to a point of feeling relief. Soon enough, I usually hear the good news that my flight is going to work out."

"Again, you inwardly focus consistently to maintain a feeling of relief, of positive emotion," God adds.

"Even recently, I was 'playing with you' and said I'd like to see a ball with the word *love* spelled out on it. I just wanted to see if it would happen and have a reminder of how connected we are," I say.

"And what happened?" God asks.

"I was on a business trip in Vancouver and had gone to dinner with a couple of friends. As we were walking back to the hotel, we passed a small shop. It was nighttime and the shop was closed, but a couple of small lamps lit up the front window. As we walked by, out of the corner of my eye I saw a large ball. So I backed up and looked in the window, and saw a large 4- to 5-foot inflatable ball with the word LOVE spelled out in large 1-foot letters, and off to the side was a smaller ball with the word LOVE across it. It made me really smile and feel good. So thanks for that," I say.

"You're welcome," God says. "How does it feel right now remembering all these things that have worked out for you?"

"Good, I feel good," I say.

"And why do you feel better, why does remembering all the ways life works out for you make you feel better?"

"Because when I focus on all the good that I have and appreciate it, this is aligned with my inherent God nature so I feel good, positive. How's that?" I say.

"Great! Right now, in this moment, you didn't need any outer condition to change for you to be able to feel better; it is an inner journey, remember that," God says.

"So that is another way to align with your inherent God nature and align yourself vibrationally and emotionally: simply deliberately recall and revisit all the good that has occurred in your life. Revisit and think upon and feel all the times life has worked out, and realize that it was because you used your inherent God nature to manifest all these things. You have manifested tons that have worked out for you, so use that to stay aligned and feel good too," God reminds me.

"With all these things and others you are indicating that you can consistently keep your emotional and vibrational focus, meaning you keep focusing on and thinking consistently about what you want and more easily feel the doneness of it in present time, but not with something like money."

"What is it about money that makes it difficult to maintain your vibrational focus?" God asks.

"I don't really know."

"Is your sense of well-being and feeling secure in life tied up with manifesting the car or the house, for example?"

"Not at all," I say. "With the car, I guess it doesn't really matter to me if I have that car or not. Heck, my first two cars were used cars that cost me a total of $800. I didn't really need a new car; I just really wanted one. So the whole process of visualizing was fun. Same with the house."

"That's important," God says. "With a car or your house, you don't have any big attachment to the outcome. You don't have a strong sense of 'needing it' and believing your well-being is impacted whether you have it or not."

"But it feels like I really need money. It feels more urgent, like my survival is at stake, my well-being is at risk, the outcome does matter," I reply.

"Think about beliefs such as 'If I don't have enough money my well-being or survival is at risk' or 'Money is difficult,' or 'I'm not worthy of it' or 'Money is evil,' God says. "Do any of these sound familiar?"

"Sure; they all do," I say.

"And how do you feel whenever you focus and think like this and believe in this way?"

"Well fear, worry and concern kick in," I admit.

"And the law of consciousness, the law of attraction is responding to the vibrational frequencies," God says. "Any of these false or limiting beliefs should and will cause you to feel things like 'urgent, desperate, worry, concern, and fear.' Again, this focus and type of thinking is not aligned with what your inherent God nature knows to be true about your well-being and survival and abundance, so you feel the 'offness' of it. You feel negative emotions. And again, these emotions have nothing to do with money itself; they have to do with your focus and thinking not being aligned with what your inherent God knows to be true," God says, reminding me of what my emotions mean.

"But you have come to accept these false and limiting beliefs as real. You have repeated them and embodied and practiced them so frequently that they have become chronic patterns of thought and chronic ways to feel; therefore, these false or limiting beliefs have also become chronic vibrational patterns that law of consciousness, law of attraction, the law of your being is responding to. As a result, you keep manifesting problems with money.

"Think about getting a bill or your mortgage payment. When you are experiencing a chronic pattern like this, it happens quickly, BAM! You start to worry in what seems like an instant. You still go through the process of focusing, but you have thinking that is not aligned with your inherent God nature, and you feel worry, but it happens instantaneously because it is so practiced and is a chronic pattern. It is as if your body and nervous system simply do it for you without you having to give it much active thought."

Reason Two

God claps his hands again, and two loud roars of thunder roll across the sky. "Here is another important reason you struggle to manifest what you want: Having false or limiting beliefs that you continue to focus on and perceive as true, real, factual, known are vibrationally kept active.

"Knowing means you have embodied a belief (any belief) to a point that it is fully accepted and KNOWN within you, within your consciousness, within your being. It is factual to you. You have fully accepted it, even if it is a way of thinking, a belief, that is false and limits you.

"You have done this with beliefs that serve you and beliefs that limit you. But in both situations, over time or perhaps sometimes immediately, you took a thought, repeated it enough for it to become a thought with feeling, which became a belief. Then that belief over time became FELT and KNOWN in your being, in your consciousness; therefore, it is vibrationally active.

"But remember," God continues, *"conditions are drawn to your known and embodied beliefs, not to you personally. You are not your beliefs. You simply have embodied beliefs unawarely that do not serve you or others."*

*It is not what you want that you
attract; you attract what you
believe to be true.*

Neville Goddard,
The Art of Believing

"These are like stations on the radio that you keep tuning to. You don't have to, but you are in the habit of doing so. You are not stuck with this, and you don't have to tune in to them," God says.

"What happened the other day when you were mowing your grass?" I think back for a moment.

"I was mowing, but I was feeling discouraged. I felt like a failure and that things in my life were not working out the way I wanted, and I wasn't doing enough," I admit.

"So old false and limiting beliefs were active, it sounds like," God says.

"Yes, and it sucked."

"But what did you do?"

"I stopped myself and began reminding myself that this was only old false beliefs. I did it as a way to shift my focus and my thinking; I began appreciating what was around me instead. I began appreciating my back yard and actually having a yard to mow. I appreciated that I could walk and push my mower. I had just visited my dad, who can't walk on his own anymore without a walker or wheelchair. I appreciated having this house and all the good in my life, and I started to feel better within a few minutes."

"It might not feel like magic, but this is one of the ways you stop and interrupt your old false and limiting beliefs. You didn't just say a positive thought, you genuinely took the time to think and find thoughts until you felt better. Changing yourself emotionally and therefore vibrationally was the goal. As you do this you come to embody the new belief," God says.

"You can interrupt old false and limiting beliefs while you practice embodying new beliefs that do serve you and others and get in the habit of tuning in to them. This is what you did while mowing your lawn."

I start laughing. God looks at me. "What's funny?"

"The old 4Runner we were just sitting in. I used to tape a picture of me when I was 5 years old to the dashboard. I used that image to practice believing I was worthy and to interrupt some negative thinking I had about myself. As you were talking about interrupting old beliefs while embodying new ones, I remembered doing this. I was consistent, and it made a difference and helped me change an old belief I had."

"As you mentioned, with money you continue to manifest struggles about debt but you also have more moments of abundance," God says.

"Yes, that's correct; these days I seem to manifest both," I reply.

"Then all is working out perfectly, like I said," God says.

"Well, I don't know about that. Still manifesting debt and lack doesn't sound perfect to me," I reply.

"But it is, and it is exciting. Sure, you still have an active false and limiting belief about money, but big deal; its old news. What is important is that you are beginning to spend enough time and attention focusing on a new belief about abundance! Good deal and great news!" God says excitedly.

"You are being consistent with your inner work of focusing your thinking to align more and more with your inherent God nature on the subject of money, and as a result, you are shifting yourself vibrationally toward more abundance and manifesting more abundance. You really are doing all of it simply through the power of your focus and your attention. *You are God consciousness, focusing within God consciousness, so your focus has the ability to activate consciousness and ultimately manifest physical conditions that match it either positively or negatively.*"

"So what do I need to do about the limiting beliefs I have?" I ask.

"Well, they seem to work pretty well," God jokes. "Meaning that over time, you focused and repeatedly thought a certain way about money. Yes, you learned this from external life but regardless of how it came to be, it made its way within you and *was fully accepted by you.* You came to feel about and ultimately believe in things such as, 'my survival depends on money,' and 'I might not make it.' This repetition eventually allowed you to embody this belief to a point to which it feels like a 'fact' to you and therefore 'known' to you, which has a frequency and vibration and attracts conditions to match it."

"So can I make it not work? Can I stop the limiting belief from vibrating and being active so I stop attracting conditions of lack?" I ask.

"It is much easier than that," God says. "You can simply activate what you want. You can activate a belief that benefits you and others and come to KNOW this belief as real and true, and embody it just like you did the false or limiting belief."

> *If there are things in your experience that you no longer wish to experience, your belief must change. If there are things that are not in your experience that you want to bring into your experience, your belief must change.*
>
> Ester and Jerry Hicks,
> *Ask and It Is Given*

"And you are already doing this with the subject of money. You are consistently journaling to focus yourself, to focus your thoughts on abundance, and you are doing it to the point you feel better. Sometimes you do this inwardly and sometimes you speak it out loud and let yourself feel the truth of it.

"You are deliberately blessing your money and bills each time you pay them. You give freely and easily when it feels right to do so. You keep visualizing yourself financially free, debt free, and you practice the inherent feeling of joy and appreciation of being abundant. You stop yourself when you notice you are worrying and shift your thinking, which shifts how you feel. You do not let yourself just hang out endlessly in worry or concern. So as a result of all of this, you are having more positive feelings about money and the financial conditions in your life are letting you know it. You are shifting your consciousness to align with the consciousness of your inherent God nature; therefore, conditions are shifting also."

"And the truth shall set you free..." I say out loud. "I've heard that many times before, but it has a newer meaning for me as we talk about this. My old truth was that I had to have debt; the newer truth I'm embodying is one of abundance and being financially free. The law of attraction, law of consciousness is responding to my new truth."

For several years I had been feeling called to find a financial advisor, but I kept ignoring the urge and putting it off. While writing this book I decided to ask God for a financial advisor. I began to fully appreciate this advisor and thank them for their work and guidance before finding them. Within in a couple of weeks, I got a message from a cousin I do not see or talk to often. He now works for a financial advisor and wanted to know if I would be willing to come and meet the person he works for and hear what they do. I couldn't help but smile, send a "thank you" to God, and say yes. Learning about and getting my finances in shape has been a real blessing, and I love that I now have this advisor helping me.

"What do you think would happen if you were to be even more consistent? If you only blessed money, appreciated money, only reached for feelings of well-being, joy, and love through the consistent and deliberate focus of your attention and thinking? Only thought, felt and spoke well of money, easily gave money and easily received it, and only felt good about it? What would happen if you stopped yourself every time your focus and feelings about money became negative, and you deliberately shifted your focus and attention and purposely generated better feelings about it?" God asks.

"I really think I would continuously feel good about money and consistently feel secure and have a sense of well-being," I say.

"Yes; exactly, and what would happen to the limiting belief of money and old negative feelings around it?" God asks.

"I'm not sure, but if I'm not focusing on them then I'm not activating them, so I'm not sure it would actually really matter what happens to them," I say.

God smiles. "True, it really doesn't matter because you aren't activating them any longer. You are not continuing to shift radio stations. You are maintaining your vibrational focus on the subject of money and doing it in a way that aligns with what your inherent God nature knows about money and abundance. Your positive feelings and emotions let you know this. You strengthen your 'focusing muscle' to stay focused and perceive what you want, and what you don't want falls away. You can do this with all things.

"Can you analyze your old beliefs and explore how they came to be without focusing on them?" God asks.

"Well no, that would be impossible," I say.

"Right," God says. "You can't deliberately focus on a limiting belief and not activate it at the same time. Your focused attention to something activates consciousness. Stay focused on the new belief and the old will take care of itself.

"Giving these false and limiting beliefs your focus, attention and feeling is how they became ingrained and embodied in the first place. So it is okay to be honest with yourself and acknowledge negative beliefs you are aware of. Know they are there, but I caution you not to spend too much time talking about them and analyzing how they came to be, because you can't talk about them without continuing to focus on them, which keeps them active. Realize the belief, and then move on to what you want! Start embodying the belief that serves you, to the point of truly knowing it within your being.

"A quick way to really know whether a belief you have is limiting you is to simply pay attention to how you feel or look around at the conditions in your life. A belief you have about yourself that makes you feel negative is a false or limiting belief. The negative feelings are always an indicator for you, and so are the negative conditions in your personal life. I say *personal* because certain conditions have to do with your group consciousness as a collection of people on the planet, but there are also conditions that have to do with you, and these are what we have been discussing," God says.

I am not telling you to inhibit thoughts or feelings. I am asking that you become aware of those you have. Realize that they form your reality. Concentrate upon those that give you the results that you want.

If you find all of this difficult, you can also examine your physical reality in all of its aspects. Realize that your physical experience and environment is the materialization of your beliefs.

If you find great exuberance, health, effective work, abundance, smiles on the faces of those you meet, then take it for granted that your beliefs are beneficial. If you see a world that is good, people that like you, take it for granted, again, that your beliefs are beneficial.

But if you find poor health, a lack of meaningful work, a lack of abundance, a world of sorrow and

evil, then assume that your beliefs
are faulty and begin
examining them.

Jane Roberts, *Seth Speaks*

God takes my hand. "I'm always holding steady your new improved version of you; this you that you are deciding you want to be. There is nothing static about God, consciousness, God consciousness; all are dynamic, expansive and eternal. So, as you desire something new, this new version of you is now held in consciousness, real in consciousness, alive and well in consciousness, vibrationally real. Your job is always to allow it and embody it so you can then experience it physically. Again, you do this by knowing it...by aligning with your inherent God nature and this inner place of wholeness and completeness...by consistently practicing the feeling and knowingness of this new version of you with your desire complete. First, embodied within yourself, within your consciousness then experienced outside next."

Reason Three

God claps his hands again and three loud roars of thunder rumble across the sky. "A third thing that gets in your way of manifesting what you want is having an underlying feeling of trying to force things, trying to will the conditions to manifest, trying to 'make something happen' during your prayer and visualizing time. Have you ever noticed moments like these when you visualize about money?"

I think for a moment. "I do sometimes feel like I shift to trying to 'make it happen.' It is subtle, but if I'm being honest I do start to feel myself struggle or like I'm trying to force the manifestation to happen, to will it to happen while I'm visualizing," I admit.

"Even when you were manifesting the 4Runner you were not trying to make it happen. You were participating in the process but not trying to control it or the outcome. You were seeing it done and feeling it done; you were enjoying and appreciating it done, but you were mainly feeling joy and appreciation and letting the process be. No interference; you were not visualizing and trying to control the law of consciousness, law of attraction to make it happen," God says. "You were simply having fun shifting your consciousness."

"Think back to times when you were in prayer and were visualizing yourself with abundance, free of debt. This focus aligns with your inherent God nature, and you started feeling a bit of relief; you felt good, with an appreciation for money and what it feels like to be debt-free," God says. I start recalling some of these times.

He whispers something to me. I can't really hear what he says, and I lean in a bit closer. He whispers again, even lower this time. I still can't hear what He says. I cup my hand behind my ear and lean in a bit closer. God whispers again, "If you really tune in to how you feel during some of your prayer and meditation times you will feel this nuance, this subtle shift, and you will notice that somewhere along the way you stopped feeling positive, or maybe you never felt positive to begin with, and you start feeling more tense or anxious about it. When your feelings start to become negative, even slightly, is when you tend to try to will the condition to change. So it is important for you to keep an inner ear tuned to paying attention to how you feel as you do your inner work, like visualizing or praying.

"Knowing there is abundance and feeling as though you need to make things happen are two very different vibrational signals in consciousness. Genuinely knowing and feeling joy and appreciation of abundance vibrationally aligns with more conditions of abundance," God says.

- "Feeling that you need to make it happen means you are no longer focused on 'knowing' it is done in consciousness.
- On some level, you are doubting and not trusting. These feelings mean your focus has shifted to the unwanted condition.

- Once you start doubting or not trusting you then inwardly or outwardly try to 'make it happen' or force it instead.
- You are visualizing but you are no longer focused on shifting consciousness; you are now focused on shifting the condition, and in some way trying to control the law of consciousness, law of attraction too."

"Simply realize that while you pray and visualize you can't feel struggle and try to will the condition to manifest, to make it happen, and at the same time fully know it is done and feel the joy and love and appreciation of it. As I mentioned, you are always dealing with consciousness and not conditions. However, some conditions truly grab your attention to a point that you feel fear, worry, and dread. With some of these conditions, you fear as if your well-being or survival is at risk," God says. "When you fear your well-being or survival is at risk is when you tend to do this more often."

"I think for me, God, this happens with issues of money and physical or health issues," I say.

"Physical health issues are challenging for you because you live in this physical body now, and you get very attached to it and perceive it as your true self as opposed to realizing that your true self is your inherent God nature, which simply resides within this physical body for a period of time. Your physical body is a manifested condition.

"With physical health issues, you shift your focus, perhaps unconsciously, and believe more in the realness of the physical condition than in the power of your inherent God nature. In these moments, *you believe that conditions cause life and forget that the consciousness you activate by power of your focused attention (awarely or unawarely) attract the physical conditions in your life.*

"You also forget the power and influence you have to shift the conditions. You forget what your fear or worry really means. Once this happens, you tend to focus on really needing and wanting the condition to shift. It can be subtle, but urgency sets in and even though you are in prayer and visualizing, you begin to will the conditions to change and try to make it happen. This leads you to intensify your focus on the unwanted condition. As you intensify your focus on the unwanted condition, you also intensify your negative emotions, and you get a pretty good vibrational thing going," God explains. I easily recall moments of this happening.

"Of course, by law you get even more of the unwanted condition you are so desperately trying to change."

*It is a fact that the struggle ceases
as fast as you can eliminate
struggle out of consciousness; the
very struggle after the thing is the
thing that keeps the thing
away from you.*

Earnest Holmes, *Love and Law*

"So at these times, back up a moment and stop
trying to visualize the improved condition; instead,
simply try to feel better. Reach for thoughts that
reassure you of your inherent God nature and that
align with your inherent God nature. Remind yourself
that it is your consciousness you need to deal with,
not the condition," God says.

"It's hard, you know, to do this when the condition
seems too strong and powerful and real and
threatening," I tell God. "Both my mom and my best
friend died of cancer, and I was very blessed to be
with them each day during their last few weeks and
when they died. Everything you are sharing feels true
to me, but it is harder to accept and practice when
someone is dealing with a physical illness like the
ones they had. I've not personally had to practice
this with an illness such as cancer, but I have read
about many who have. I once read a book called *You
Are the Placebo* by Dr. Joe Dispenza, and he shares
his story of overcoming an injury. In his book, there

are many stories of others who have overcome illnesses by shifting their consciousness." I find all of their stories inspiring and am thankful for them.

"I understand it can be more challenging to shift your consciousness with physical issues and easy for fear to kick in," God says. "Yet, the intensity of your fear is simply an indicator of how removed your perception, thinking, and believing are from your inherent God nature in those moments. Your intense fear is not about the condition."

"You're right," I say, "I do forget what my feelings mean at those times when I feel intense fear.

"If it is hard to truly believe the health issue is improved in nonphysical consciousness because you physically feel it, and you are feeling fearful, then work to interrupt how you are thinking and therefore feeling," God says.

"Make an active decision to think differently in order to feel some sort of relief. Become more generalized about the issue; go through the back door, so to speak. Begin by reminding yourself how well your body does heal things. Remind yourself that more of your body is healthy than is sick. Remind yourself that your cells are brilliant and intelligent. Or if all you can do is send love and love and more love to your body and appreciate it, then do that. Any of this type of thinking and focus will feel better because it

aligns with your inherent God nature. Use this type of thinking and focus to work your way toward fully accepting your desire complete and known, to feeling it complete and done. Or do your best to get quiet and be still and go to silence, and focus on being with your inherent nature that is well, whole and complete, and hang out there to soak in the good vibes. Or go in a completely different direction and get your mind onto something else. Watch your favorite comedies and laugh as much as possible.

"Regardless of the issue that grabs your attention, the quick fix to interrupting 'trying to will the conditions to change and make it happen' is to pay more attention to how you feel while you do your inner work. If while you are praying and visualizing you are having fun and feeling good then you are on the right track. If you start to feel you are trying to 'make it happen,' stop yourself and stop your visualization time. Get your mind on something else that will help you just feel better overall, regardless of the subject, and try again later. Remember, I manifest life for the joy of life, the joy of creating. Reach for those feelings as you do your work. Be patient with you, be kind to yourself," God adds.

I feel encouraged as I listen. I know I can be more consistent; I know I can focus on what I want and activate beliefs that serve others and me and do it to a point of knowing. I know I can use my feelings to let me know whether I have a false or limiting belief getting in my way. I also know I can become more aware of when I am trying to make things happen and intervene and shift how I am using my power of focus and attention.

I clap my hands. Nothing. No thunder. I do it again, still nothing. God laughs and looks at me. "I had to try!" I say.

I feel a bit of a stir in the air again. Then we are at the beach. It is still quiet, with a slight breeze, and we are sitting in the sand and the waves wash over my feet. God leans into me, shoulder to shoulder, and our heads lightly touch. I feel silence for a moment, a warmth. God whispers to me the following:

- "Remember, you are an extension of God consciousness. You are my wave and I am the ocean. I love each one of you. Yes, even those you struggle with.
- "You exist here and now in God consciousness, which is an alive, awake, intelligent and loving consciousness.
- "You are this God consciousness in both physical and nonphysical form.
- "You can never be separate from me, from God, and your God nature cannot be extracted from you. It is given and done

forever. Relax and breathe a bit. Lighten up a bit.

- "I create from a place of wholeness and completeness. I do not create because of lack or need of any kind. Lack did not inspire me to create life. Lack did not inspire creation. Love did.

- "Yet, you can manifest conditions of lack, and you have. This doesn't make 'lack' a true and real thing, only a manifested condition that you have unawarely mistaken as real and true.

- "Any technique you use to manifest is about you and about you allowing yourself to become the new version of consciousness, which contains you and your desire complete. None of your techniques or prayer are about me. I do not need convincing, and if you are doing any of these to get me to do something then you are missing the mark.

- "Belief in lack inspires fear, and yes, you can create from fear but you tend to not like the outcome.

- "I created you and others and life for the fun of life, for the joy of life, for the appreciation of life, for the act of creating and expressing. When you are full of life, full of love, you naturally want to express it. You already do this to some degree.

- "Because you are an expression of me, you too can create with and in consciousness.
- "You have within you the power to activate consciousness by the power and focus of your attention and thought.
- "By combining consistent focus or consistent thought and generating emotion and feeling, these ingredients allow you to embody any belief you choose and create a vibration, a signal, a frequency.
- "And the law of your being, of consciousness, of attraction draws to you like conditions.
- "All is well and all is always truly well. Do not believe in the conditions of life more than your true inherent God nature."

The world is saturated with
Divinity, immersed in Reality, and
filled with possibility.

Earnest Holmes,
The Science of Mind

As we continue to sit there, I hear the waves and feel the breeze and there is a pause. More silence. All feels good. All is good. Then I continue to hear God whisper, "I AM is my name. I AM is consciousness. I AM is God consciousness. I AM has power. You are also 'I AM'. Your 'I AM' has power. Use it wisely." I want to ask about the 'I Am' but I know that conversation will have to come later.

I hear the sounds of prayer bells. One ring, two rings, three rings. I realize those bells mean my prayer time for now has ended.

AMEN

61767282R00080

Made in the USA
Lexington, KY
19 March 2017